LONDON MADE EASY

Paul Tarrant

Author of *England & Wales Guide*

Open Road Publishing

Open Road Publishing

We offer travel guides to American and foreign locales. Our books tell it like it is, often with an opinionated edge, and our experienced authors always give you all the information you need to have the trip of a lifetime. Write for your free catalog of all our titles.

Open Road Publishing
P.O. Box 284, Cold Spring Harbor, NY 11724
E-mail: Jopenroad@aol.com

ABOUT THE AUTHOR

Paul Tarrant is a freelance writer and the author of Open Road Publishing's *England & Wales Guide*. Paul makes his home in Bournemouth, England.

TABLE OF CONTENTS

Maps

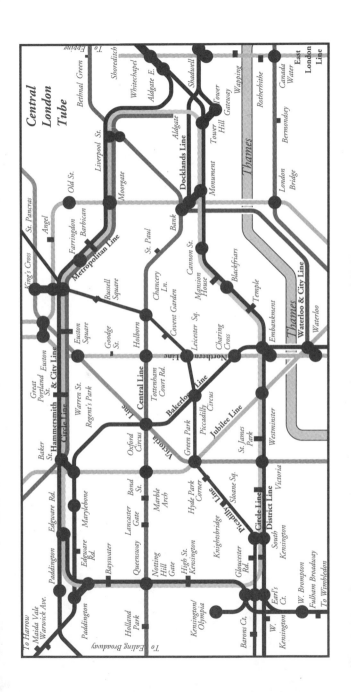

Central London Tube

INTRODUCTION

London is one of the world's most captivating cities and just oozes history and culture. You'll be bowled over by its fantastic museums and galleries, dazzling shops and pulsating nightlife and by the glorious parks and gardens which make it the world's greenest capital. Around every corner you'll find something new and interesting to grab your attention, from medieval churches to royal palaces; pubs where Dickens used to drink to stunning modern constructions like the Millennium Wheel. And let's not forget the pomp and pageantry that London is famous for – from the Changing of the Guard ceremony to the grand parades and processions of the City of London.

And while some may scoff at the idea of London as a gourmet destination, those with epicurean savvy will know that some of the world's finest chefs – and restaurants – are located here.

Because London is such a vast, sprawling metropolis, finding your way around the city is not always easy. The aim of this little guide is to take away some of the confusion. Tuck our book into your pocket and you'll have London at your fingertips, from familiar sights like Big Ben and the Tower of London, to the unusual Tea and Coffee Museum, with tips on places to shop and where to eat, covering all price brackets.

If you only have a few days in London, we'll make it easy for you to truly experience the city, rather than spending all your time in queues. We've also included some interesting walks: Explore the streets and alleyways of Whitechapel, haunt of Jack the Ripper, or tour the theaters of the West End; imbibe the villagey atmosphere of Hampstead or visit some of the places familiar to the late Diana, Princess of Wales.

You may get tired *by* London, but you'll never be tired *of* London. We're convinced that whether you're here for just a few days or a few weeks this handy little pocket guide to London is all you need to make your visit enjoyable, rewarding – and easy.

1. SIGHTS

With around seven million inhabitants, and covering around 650 square miles, London is easily the largest city in Europe. At first, it may all seem a bit overwhelming – there's just so much to see and do. We cover the main attractions, but we've also added a sprinkling of lesser-known sights that will intrigue, and even surprise, you.

High on your list of priorities must be the **Tower of London**, the ancient fortress built by William the Conqueror and home of the **Crown Jewels**. Then there's **Westminster Abbey,** built way back in 1065, where British monarchs have been crowned for centuries and, nearby, the **Houses of Parliament** and **Big Ben**. Listen to the choir of **St Paul's Cathedral** - scene of the wedding of Prince Charles to the late Princess Diana in 1971.

Don't miss the mind-blowing **British Museum**, one of the most extensive collections of art and artifacts in the world; **the Victoria and Albert Museum,** the best fine arts museum on the planet, and the **Natural History Museum** where you'll be greeted by an 80ft long diplodocus as you enter.

The world-famous **National Gallery**, the fabulous new **Tate Modern Gallery** at Bankside and the rebuilt Shakespeare **Globe Theatre** are all within your grasp. If it's blood and gore you want, then the **London Dungeon** is for you, though you might get even more of a kick out of **Madame Tussaud's**, with its famous Chamber of Horrors, or the **Old Operating Theatre**, with its blood-curdling collection of implements used in surgical operations long bevore the advent of anaesthetics Stroll in beautiful **Hyde Park** and visit the controversial new **Diana Memorial Fountain**, or adjacent **Kensington Gardens** with the newly restored memorial to Prince Albert, Queen Victoria's other half, glittering with lashings of gold leaf. Walk past the stately buildings of **Whitehall**, the nation's political heart, to **Trafalgar Square**. For retail therapy **Oxford Street**, the world's busiest shopping street, can't be beat - but don't forget **Knightsbridge**, home of Harrods, **Bond Street** and the warren of chic shopping streets between Oxford Street and Piccadilly.

Outside of the West End and City (the name given to the city's main financial district) London is made up of countless "villages" each with its own distinctive character and style; like **Hampstead** and **Highgate** in north London, and **Chelsea**, to the south west. There's even more to see on the outskirts of the metropolis: **Windsor Castle**, west of London, is the Queen's favorite residence while **Hampton Court Palace**, built by Henry VIII for Cardinal Wolsey and snatched back by the greedy king, is perhaps the most architecturally pleasing of all the royal residences.

This is a truly great city; whether you're here for just a few days or a few weeks you won't fail to be captivated by it. You may get tired *by* it, but you'll never be tired *of* it. And maybe, just maybe, you'll end up agreeing with Dr. Johnson who famously said, "When a man is tired of London, he is tired of life."

BUS TOURS
The Original London Sightseeing Tour
Tel. 020 8877 1722
www.theoriginaltour.com
Evan Evans Tours
Tel. 020 7950 1777
www.evanevans.co.uk
Back-Roads Touring Company
Tel. 020 8566 5312
www.backroadstouring.co.uk
Green Line
Tel. 020 8688 7261
www.greenline.co.uk
Original Tours
Tel. 0208 877 1722
www.theoriginaltour.com

Westminster, Whitehall, & The Palace

The Tate Britain
Millbank, London SW1
Tel. 0207 887 8008
Open year-round daily 10am to 5:30pm
Admission: free (but donations welcome)
Nearest Tube: Pimlico

The Tate Gallery on Millbank has been a repository of post-1500 **British art** and **international modern art** for well over a century, but never more than a small fraction of the collection was ever on display because of its limited gallery space. In the 1990s, work started on converting a disused power station on Bankside, south of the River, into a massive new gallery to house the modern art collection – the **Tate Modern**, while the collection of British art remained at the old Tate, now called the **Tate Britain**. Amazingly, admission to both galleries is free (though donations are welcome). During the summer, a special free ArtBus links the two galleries between 10am and 6pm.

The Tate Britain holds the largest collection of British art in the world, with works by Blake, Constable, Epstein, Hockney, Hogarth and Rossetti. Like the National Gallery, the volume of works on show is staggering, and you may need more than one visit. Among the Tate's highlights are William Hogarth's *O The Roast Beef of Old England* and *Satan, Sin and Death*, several works by famous 18th century British artists Sir Joshua Reynolds and Sir Thomas Gainsborough, and a collection of works by J.M. Turner, left to the nation by the artist himself and displayed in the new Clore Gallery. There's a room dedicated to another great British landscape artist, John Constable.

The Tate Gallery **restaurant** is a work of art in itself; an elegant dining room decorated with murals by Rex Whistler, while the adjacent cafe serves cakes, croissants, sandwiches and salads at reasonable prices.

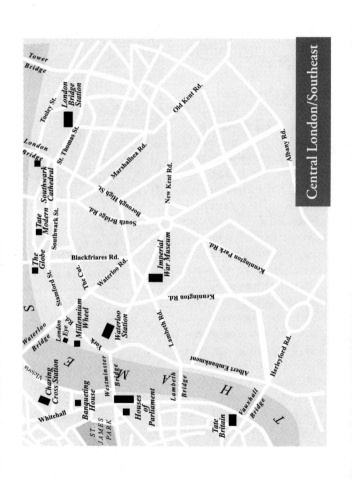

Central London/Southeast

Tower Bridge

Tooley St.

London Bridge Station

Old Kent Rd.

St. Thomas St.

London Bridge

Southwark Cathedral

Marshallsea Rd.

New Kent Rd.

Albany Rd.

Tate Modern

Southwark St.

Borough High St.

South Bridge Rd.

Kennington Park Rd.

The Globe

Blackfriares Rd.

Imperial War Museum

Stamford St.

The Cut

Waterloo Rd.

Kennington Rd.

S

London Eye

Millennium Wheel

York Rd.

Waterloo Station

Lambeth Rd.

Herteford Rd.

Waterloo Bridge

E

Albert Embankment

Victoria

Charing Cross Station

Westminster Bridge

M

V

Lambeth Bridge

H

Banqueting House

Houses of Parliament

Whitehall

ST. JAMES PARK

Tate Britain

Vauxhall Bridge

I

Westminster Cathedral
Victoria Street, W1
Tel. 0207 798 9055
www.westminstercathedral.org.uk
Open daily 7am to 7pm.
Admission: free
Tower open April to November
9am to 5pm, December to
March Thursday to Sunday
9am to 5pm
Admission to Tower: £2
Nearest Tube: Victoria.

London's largest – and most important – Roman Catholic church dates from as recent as 1903. It's is a fantastic example of neo-Byzantine architecture. The redbrick pile is banded with Portland stone stripes and a 273ft campanile provides visitors with a bird's eye view over Westminster – thankfully there's an elevator. The **interior** was never completed, but that makes the place even more atmospheric. The imposing nave is England's widest, and the walls are covered with more than 100 different marbles from around the world. Pope John Paul II celebrated mass here in 1982.

Westminster Abbey
Dean's Yard, SW1
Tel. 0207 222 5152
www.westminster-abbey.org
Open Monday to Friday
9.20am to 3.45pm, Saturday

RESTAURANT TIP
Rhodes in the Square
Dolphin Square
Chichester Street, SW1
Tel: 0207 798 6767
Nearest Tube: Pimlico

Gary Rhodes, one of the UK's best known TV chefs, owns this place, which might explain its popularity. Only the freshest British ingredients are used. It's certainly not cheap, but a real treat. ✻

9am to 1.45pm
Admission Royal Chapels, nave and cloisters adults £5, children £2; Abbey Museum, Pyx Chamber and Chapter House £1 extra.
Nearest Tube: Westminster

Saxon **King Edward** (later venerated and known as "The Confessor") founded the Abbey in 1065, when it was part of a **Benedictine** monastery. Harold was crowned king here in 1066, as was his vanquisher, **William of Normandy**, and just about every other monarch (except Edward V and Edward VIII) since. It's an impressive building and very much the "**national church**". So cluttered with tombs and monuments to the great and good is it, that it sometimes seems more like a museum than a place of worship. It has also been the setting for countless **national events** – the weddings and funerals of kings and queens, and of course, more recently the moving funeral service for Diana, Princess of Wales.

The present building dates mostly from the 13th and 14th centuries, a rebuild of Edward's original 11th century construction. The twin towers at the west end are much later; they were designed by **Sir Christopher Wren**, and added in the 17th century.

Entering by the west door, the **nave**, with its elegant rib-vaulting spreads out before you as far as the intricately-gilded choir screen. Beyond this lies one of the highlights of the Abbey, **the Henry VII Chapel**. Close to the main west door is the **Tomb of the Unknown Warrior**, an anonymous World War I soldier, while just a few paces away is the marble slab memorial to **Sir Winston Churchill**; his funeral service took place here in 1965.

Pass through into the **choir** area, with its 19th century stalls,

and into the **North Transept**. The **Rose Window** here is one of the largest in Britain. To proceed further, into the Henry VII Chapel and beyond, you'll need to pay an additional admission charge, but it's worth it. The Chapel, with more fine rib-vaulting, carvings and sculptures, has been described as "the finest in Christendom." Here, you can see the white marble tomb of **Elizabeth I**, buried with her half-sister **Mary I**.

Further on is the **Chapel of Edward the Confessor**. Next to the saint's shrine stands the **Coronation Chair**, where many monarchs have been crowned. The Stone of Scone, which had graced the chair for centuries, was recently returned to Scotland, its original home.

Another focal point for visitors is **Poets' Corner**, with monuments to just about every British literary luminary, starting with Chaucer, and including Shakespeare, Tennyson, Hardy and Dylan Thomas.

Other Abbey attractions worth at least a peep are the 13th century **Chapter House**, and the **Museum**, located in the Norman undercroft with a motley collection of artefacts including wax effigies, old religious vestments and ancient documents.

For choral music of the highest quality, attend an **evensong service** at Westminster Abbey, St Paul's Cathedral or Southwark Cathedral, where you can hear world-class men and boys choirs for free. You don't have to be an Episcopalian – or even a Christian – to attend, but you'll be sure of an uplifting experience whatever your persuasion. There's also a fine choir at Westminster Roman Catholic Cathedral. Check the times in the Sunday papers.

The Houses of Parliament
Parliament Square, SW1
Tel. 0207 219 4272
www.parliament.uk
Hours vary, depending on when parliament is in session. Guided tours during summer recess early August to late September Monday to Saturday 9.15am to 7.30pm
Admission (tour): £3.50
Nearest Tube: Westminster

Just across the road from Westminster Abbey are Houses of Parliament, dwarfed by the 363' high St Stephen's Tower and Big Ben – not the name of the clock but of the bell that strikes the hour. This was the site of the Royal Palace of Westminster, where kings and queens lived until they moved to Whitehall. The present building, designed by the architect Pugin, dates from 1840, replacing an earlier building that was burned down in the 1830s. It was heavily bombed during World War II.

PARIS MADE EASY?

You can be in the French capital in a mere three hours. The Eurostar train speeds you through the French and English countryside and through the Channel Tunnel (the "Chunnel"), allowing you to visit Paris and London in the same day. You leave London's Waterloo Station and arrive in Paris's Gare du Nord. Fares are around £120 (one-way), £180 (round-trip second class), £200 (one-way first class) and £300 (round-trip first class). Contact Eurostar, *Tel. 800/EUROSTAR, www.eurostar.co.uk.* For more information on visiting Paris, pick up Open Road's *Paris Made Easy.*

The two Houses, the House of Commons, where 650 MPs (Members of Parliament) sit, is shaped like a chapel, and the two major political parties face each other 'across the benches'. Debates can be fiery, with constant heckling provoking the Speaker to cry "Order, order!" The adjacent House of Lords is a more sedate affair. It has undergone considerable constitutional reforms under Tony Blair's government and hereditary peers no longer have an automatic right to sit here.

The two Houses of Parliament are in general closed to the public, but it is possible to watch a debate from the Strangers' Gallery, though it may involve a long wait in line. US or Canadian citizens can expedite things by getting a special pass from the US Embassy or Canadian High Commission but they can only issue a measly four tickets a day.

Whitehall
Nearest Tube: Westminster or Charing Cross

Lined with stately government buildings, Whitehall, site of the ancient royal **Palace of Whitehall**, leads from Trafalgar Square to Parliament Square and the Houses of Parliament. Many government departments are based here, including the **Admiralty** (home of the Royal Navy). On the right, heading towards Big Ben, **Horse Guards Parade** is where one of the Changing of the Guard ceremonies is held. The concrete monolith in the middle of the street is **The Cenotaph**, the focal point for services of remembrance to the fallen of World Wars I and II. Every year, on the Sunday closest to November 11 (the Day the WWI armistice was signed in 1918), the monarch, prime minister and other national dignitaries come here to place memorial wreaths of poppies.

Downing Street
Off Whitehall, SW1
Nearest Tube: Westminster

This unassuming street of row houses includes, at Number 10, the official London home of the Prime Minister - possibly the most famous street address in Britain. Access to the residence is limited, for obvious reasons. The Cabinet Office, where important decisions of state are taken, is on the ground floor, while the prime minister resides in an apartment on the top floor of Number 11, the official residence of the **Chancellor of the Exchequer**, the British finance minister. The reason is simple: at the time of the Labour government's election in 1997, the Chancellor was a bachelor. Tony Blair, with three children (now four) needed more space, and a deal was done.

The Banqueting House
Whitehall, SW1
Tel. 0207 930 4179
www.hrp.org.uk
Open Monday to Saturday 10am to 5pm
Admission: £3.50
Nearest Tube: Westminster

Inigo Jones (1573-1652) created this banqueting hall in 1622 from the remains of the Tudor **Palace of Whitehall**. Influenced by the Italian Palladio's work, Jones restructured the palace with great sophistication. Charles I later employed the Flemish painter Rubens to paint the ceiling. The allegorical paintings, depicting a wise king being received into heaven, were ironically the last thing Charles saw before being beheaded on a scaffold outside the building on January 30, 1649.

Cabinet War Rooms
Clive Steps, King Charles Street, SW1
Tel. 0207 930 6961
www.iwm.org.uk
Open May to September 9.30am to 6pm, October to April 10am to 6pm
Admission: free
Nearest Tube: Westminster

These dingy basement rooms, just behind Admiralty Arch, were Britain's wartime nerve centre. During the worst air raids of the Second World War, Winston Churchill, his Cabinet and his most senior staff lived and worked here, planning the war effort. Touring the site is made easy with new interactive audio guides with separate versions for primary age children and adults.

Admiralty Arch
Nearest Tube: Charing Cross

The great arch on the south west corner was constructed as recently as 1910 as part of a ceremonial route from Buckingham Palace. It opens into **The Mall** (rhymes with pal), a wide, tree-lined thoroughfare that leads past St James's Park to the Palace. The pavement here is pink/red, symbolizing a red carpet leading to the monarch's home.

St. James's Park
The Mall, SW1.
Nearest Tube: St James's Park

More ornate and much smaller than Hyde Park, St James's Park is a pretty space with its ornamental lakes and carefully-preened flower beds. It's home to hundreds of ducks and other waterfowl and on a hot day Londoners come here in their droves to peel off a few layers and bask in the sun. The view from the bridge on the lake over to Westminster, with its spires and turrets, is enchanting. The northern side of the Park is bounded by **The Mall**. This is an excellent vantage point for many of the more elaborate state parades, particularly when there is a visiting head of state.

AFTERNOON TEA
Capital Hotel
Basil Street SW3
Tel. 0207 589 5171
Pleasant small hotel.
£15.50

Connaught Hotel
Carlos Place W1
Tel. 0207 499 7070
£24 (with
champagne: £30)

Fortnum & Mason
Piccadilly W1
Tel. 0207 734 8040
Tea in the St James's
Restaurant. Price
£19.50

The Ritz
Piccadilly W1
Tel. 0207 493 8181
THE place for tea.
Book well in advance.
Full tea £32

✱

Buckingham Palace
The Mall, SW1
www.the-royal-collection.org.uk
Open August and September
9.30am to 4.30pm (call 0207
839 1377 as times are subject
to change at short notice)
Admission: £11.95
Nearest Tube: St James's Park

The Queen's central London residence was originally built

in red brick for the **Duke of Buckingham**, then purchased in 1762 by **George III** who needed space for his 15 children and courtiers. It has only housed the monarch since 1837, when **Victoria** transferred here from Kensington Palace. The palace was expanded and remodelled under **George IV**, who had always wanted to live here. He employed **John Nash**, the architect, to remodel it, but Nash overspent his budget by half a million pounds and was fired. Meantime George died, and Edward Blore completed the building, adding the familiar east front - the Portland stone façade was only added as recently as 1913.

The Palace is 360' long and contains 600 rooms, including the magnificent **State Ballroom**, scene of many a glittering state banquet, **Queen Victoria's Picture Gallery**, with paintings by Rembrandt, Van Dyck and Canaletto, and the **Throne Room**, with a pair of rather tacky pink chairs with the initials 'ER' and 'P'. The Queen and Prince Philip live in twelve rooms in the north wing, well out-of-bounds to the visitor.

The magnificent grounds, eminently suitable for walking one's corgis, are also out-of-bounds to the public, unless you've been invited to one of the garden parties where the great and the good (and the not so good) are treated to a scrumptious afternoon tea in recognition of all the good works they've been doing in their communities. You'll know if the Queen is *chez nous* by the presence (or not) of the **Royal Standard** flying above the central portico.

The Palace is not generally open to the public, but a small number of rooms are open in the summer, a practise that was started when Windsor Castle caught fire in 1992 and created an urgent need for cash.

Queen's Gallery
Buckingham Palace Road, SW1
Tel. 0207 930 4832
www.the-royal-collection.org.uk
Open Tuesday to Saturday 10am to 5pm, Sunday 2pm to 5pm.
Admission: £5
Nearest Tube: Victoria.

Just round the corner from the palace, in a former chapel accessed from Buckingham Palace Road, is the **Queen's Gallery**, with samples from what is recognized as the one of the finest private art collec-

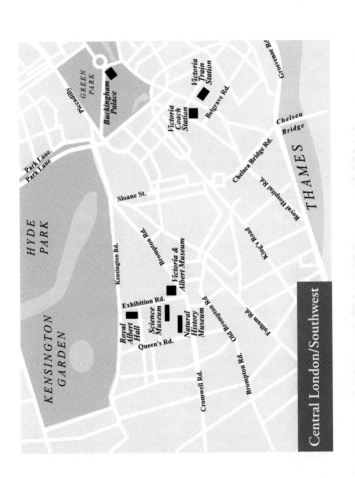

Central London/Southwest

tions in the world. See famous works like Vermeer's *The Music Lesson* and others by Rubens, Rembrandt and Canaletto, and even Queen Victoria!

Royal Mews
Buckingham Palace Road, SW1
Tel. 0207 930 4832
www.royal.gov.uk
Open April to July and October daily except Fridays 11am to 4pm; August and September daily 10am to 5pm (check exact opening days/times with Tourist Board or the websitre)
Admission: £5.50
Nearest Tube: Victoria.

A few yards further down Buckingham Palace Road is the Royal Mews, designed by John Nash. It was originally designed to house the monarch's pet falcons until horses replaced falcons as the main royal obsession. Today the Mews houses a glittering array of coaches and carriages used by the royals, including the famous **Glass Coach**, used by royal brides, and the **Irish State Coach**, used by the Queen to travel to the State Opening of Parliament. The **Gold State Coach**, used at all coronations, requires about eight horses to pull it, and is dazzling. The Mews also houses a display of historic uniforms and liveries worn by coachmen and postillions, and of course, the aristocratic gee-gees themselves.

RESTAURANT TIP
Quilan
41 Buckingham Gate, SW1
Nearest Tube: St James's Park
Tel. 0207 821 1899

Very upmarket (but what would you expect so near to the Palace?) Indian restaurant, swish décor, swish clientele. There's lots of fish and seafood on the menu which focuses on the cuisine of the Kerala region. ✽

St. James's Palace
Pall Mall, W1
Nearest Tube: Green Park

The oldest of the surviving royal palaces in London, St James's Palace is mostly Tudor, but its origins go way back to the 11th century when a hospital for female lepers stood on the site. Prince Charles resided here until 2003 when he moved to nearby **Clarence House**, which until her death had been

The Queen Mother's primary residence. Foreign ambassadors to the UK are still accredited to the 'Court of St James'. The Palace is not open to the public.

Spencer House
27 St James's Place, SW1
Tel. 0207 499 8620
www.spencerhouse.co.uk
Open February to July, September to January; Sundays only, 11.45am to 4.45pm; tours must be booked in advance – call ahead
Admission £6
Nearest Tube: Green Park

Spencer House was built in 1756-66 for John, first Earl Spencer, an ancestor of Diana, Princess of Wales, and his wife after they had eloped at his coming-of-age party. It was one of the most ambitious aristocratic town houses ever built in London and today it is the city's only great eighteenth-century private palace to survive intact. The impressive façade, adorned with neoclassical statues, best viewed through the trees of adjacent Green Park, is worth seeing in its own right, but it's the beautiful interior, designed for lavish entertaining and to house the earl's extensive collection of painting, furniture and sculpture - that really catches the eye.

The Spencers employed the best craftsmen and architects of their time. The ground floor rooms, still used during the week, include the Great Room, covered in hundreds of white, pale green and gold mosaic sections, and the **Palm Room**, designed by John Vardy, with elaborate columns carved and gilded to resemble palm trees. Upstairs, an array of stunning salons designed by James 'Athenian' Stewart affords lovely views over Green Park. The restoration of the house has been partly financed by letting out the rooms for private functions; the Queen occasionally puts on state dinners here and it was the scene of Henry Kissinger's 70th birthday bash.

Wellington Museum–Apsley House
149 Piccadilly, W1
Tel. 0207 499 5676
www.english-heritage.org.uk
Open Tuesday to Sunday 11am to 5pm
Admission: £4.50
Nearest Tube: Hyde Park Corner

Not the home of Duke Ellington, as one young student supposed, but Apsley House, London home from 1817 to 1852 of the great **Duke of Wellington**, Arthur Wellesley. He was nicknamed the 'Iron Duke' not for his military prowess, but for the iron shutters that protected the property from rioters angry at his opposition to voting reform. His successors live here today. Part of the building is open to visitors, who can admire the fine furnishings and décor, the Duke's uniforms and weapons, collections of porcelain and plate, and a large nude statue of Wellington's arch-enemy, Napoleon Bonaparte, though a (rather small) fig leaf spares his blushes. The official address of the house is 'Number One, London.'

RESTAURANT TIP
Greenhouse
27A Hays Mews, W1
Tel 020 7499 3331
Nearest Tube:
Green Park

Set back from the street in a quiet Mayfair mews, The Greenhouse made a lot of news when it opened in the early 1990s for its emphasis on British ingredients and recipes. The Brit influence is maintained in the dessert menu, which contains lots of traditional favorites like rice pudding and bread and butter pudding. Yum! ❁

Hyde Park
Nearest Tube: Hyde Park Corner

Hyde Park, central London's largest green space, was one of Henry VIII's hunting grounds. Today, its 350 acres are mostly laid to grass, with fine trees, shrubs, and a lake – the **Serpentine** – where Londoners can take a dip on hot days in the summer (and even on cold days in the winter). Take a look at nearby **Serpentine Gallery**, *(Tel 0207 402 6075; free)*, where exhibitions of modern art are on show throughout the year. The Park's southern boundary, **Rotten Row** – a corruption of the French 'Route du Roi' (route of the king), is used by the Household Cavalry, based at the nearby Knightsbridge Barracks. With its wide open expanses, Hyde Park is just perfect for flying that kite, soaking up the sun, or just chilling. It's also used for major concerts. The three tenors have sung here on a number of occasions, drawing massive crowds. For the **Princess Diana Memorial Fountain**, see Kensington, Knightsbridge and Chelsea section.

Covent Garden, Bloomsbury, & The Strand

Covent Garden Piazza
Nearest Tube: Covent Garden

The area around the old Covent Garden vegetable and flower market has undergone a total transformation since the market closed in the 1970s. New shops, restaurants and bars have burgeoned, and street entertainers do their thing in front of jolly crowds. A great place to people-watch.

St. Paul's Covent Garden
Bedford Street, WC2
Tel. 0207 836 5221
Open Monday to Friday 8.30am to 5.30pm, Sunday 9am to 1pm
Admission: free
Nearest Tube: Covent Garden

This interesting and elegant church designed by Inigo Jones was built during the reign of Charles II, and is known as the **"Actors' Church"** – its walls are littered with plaques and monuments to British actors. Commissioned by Archbishop Laud, a keen supporter of Charles I, the church was originally planned to open out onto Covent Garden Market. However, the entrance was finally created at the other end, so that the hoi polloi could not enter. Check out the memorial to Lawrence Olivier.

PUB TIP
The Lamb and Flag
33 Rose Street, WC2
Tel. 0207 836 4108
Nearest Tube:
Covent Garden

A 17th century pub with a violent history – the upstairs room was once used for bare-knuckle boxing, giving it the nickname "the Bucket of Blood." Today all that's bare are three floors, adding to the atmosphere. Things have quietened down now, and these days you can enjoy excellent lunches and real ale in peace. ✻

London Transport Museum
Covent Garden Piazza, WC2
Tel. 0207 565 7299
www.ltmuseum.co.uk
Open Saturday to Thursday 10am to 6pm, Friday 11am to 6pm
Admission: £5.95
Nearest Tube: Covent Garden

Children of all ages love the London Transport Museum in Covent Garden. There are fifteen giant hands-on KidZones with things to push and pull, lights to switch on and off, feely boxes, sliders, magnifiers and more. You'll see live actors in period costume, spectacular displays of old trams, trains and buses and even bus and tube train simulators. On a more serious note, the museum explains how London made the transition from horse-drawn carriages to the Docklands Light Railways and the new Jubilee Line extension.

Theatre Museum
7 Great Russell Street, WC2
Tel. 0207 943 4700
www.theatremuseum.org
Open Tuesday to Sunday 10am to 6pm
Admission: free
Nearest Tube: Covent Garden

Just round the corner from Covent Garden market is this colorful museum. It's an intriguing array of costume displays, artifacts and memorabilia from the stage: theater, opera and ballet, including a collection of items belonging to famous luvvies of the past. You'll also get insights into how special effects are produced. Make-up artists are on hand to explain how they do it, and if there's not too much of a queue, you might get the chance to have a makeover yourself. Who knows? You might even be asked to join the cast of *Les Miserables*.

RESTAURANT TIPS
Le Palais du Jardin
136 Long Acre, WC2
Tel 020 7379 5353
Nearest Tube:
Covent Garden.

Noisy, trendy brasserie and seafood bar: the all-French menu includes lots of seafood, with lobster a particular favorite; venison, confit of duck, and, good heavens, bangers and mash.

Porters
17 Henrietta Street, W1
Tel 0207 836 6466
Nearest Tube:
Covent Garden

English cuisine is the thing here: steak and kidney pie, jellied eels with mash roast beef and Yorkshire pudding, and spotted dick (a suet sponge smothered in jam and topped with custard). Moderately priced.

Ivy
1 West Street, WC2
Tel 020 7836 4751
Nearest Tube:
Leicester Square

Classic British dishes like braised beef in stout, haddock and chips with mushy peas prevail, and more contemporary options too.

Rules
35 Maiden Lane, WC2
Tel. 0207 836 5314
Nearest Tube:
Covent Garden

This plush 200-year-old institution has welcomed everyone from Charles Dickens to Charlie Chaplin, including royalty - the former Prince of Wales, later Edward VII, frequently brought his mistress, Lillie Langtry, here. The menu is very English. ✻

SHOPPING TIP
The Tea House
15a Neal Street, WC2

Just about every kind of tea is sold here – from orchid to Russian Caravan, not to mention an amazing array of teapots and other tea paraphernalia. ❋

Courtauld Gallery

Somerset House, The Strand, WC2
Tel. 0207 848 2526
www.courtauld.ac.uk
Open mid April to mid August 10am to 6pm; September to mid April 10am to 6pm, Sunday noon to 6pm
Admission: £4.
Nearest Tube: Temple (closed Sunday) or Embankment

Located in the north wing of the imposing Palladian-style **Somerset House**, and after a £25m refurbishment, the Courtauld displays works by the likes of Botticelli, Rubens and Velasquez. However, it's the impressionist and post-impressionist works that most people come to see, and with paintings by Van Gogh, Manet, Cezanne, Toulouse-Lautrec, Degas, Gauguin, Renoir and Monet on display who can fail to be impressed? There's also an exhibition by 20th century artists of the so-called Bloomsbury School – such as Duncan Grant, Vanessa Bell and Roger Fry.

The same building, Somerset House, is home to two other important art collections: The **Gilbert Collection** of European silver, gold snuff boxes and Italian mosaics, and the **Hermitage Rooms**, where you will find rotating displays from the Hermitage Museum in St Petersburg.

The Inns of Court

Hidden away on both sides of The Strand, the main thoroughfare between The City and Westminster, the Inns of Court – which get their name from the various inns where lawyers used to congregate - are the nucleus of legal London. Every barrister must spend some time here before qualifying. Because it escaped the ravages of the Great Fire of London, it's in a bit of a time warp, and the attractive cobbled streets and alleyways will make you feel you're in 16th century Oxford, not 21st century London.

To the north of The Strand, behind G.E. Street's monolithic **Royal Courts of Justice** (where you can watch the court proceedings from over 50 public galleries), is the oldest of the Inns of Court, **Lincoln's Inn**, on land originally given to a society of lawyers in 1287. Walking the grounds is free, but if you want to take a peek inside the halls, you'll need to call at the porter's lodge, at the entrance by Lincoln's Inn Fields. Inside the gate on the south east corner is a 17th century chapel *(open Monday to Friday noon to 2.30pm)* with a foundation stone laid by John Donne, Dean of St Paul's Cathedral in the 1600s, a member of the Hall. The **Old Hall**, built in the 15th century, has some enormous bay windows and a painting by Hogarth. Originally built to accommodate lawyers, it later became the Court of Chancery. If you've read Dickens' *Bleak House*, you'll know it as the setting for the Jarndyce vs. Jarndyce case. Close to here is Sir John Soane's Museum.

North of Lincoln's Inn, and entered from High Holborn, **Gray's Inn** (note the American spelling) is named for Sir de Grey, Chief Justice of Chester, who resided in a large house here in the 1200s. In the 1400s it served as accommodations for law students

and was extended in the 16th century. Much of it was destroyed during the Blitz and then rebuilt, but much of the **Hall** remains intact, including a wonderful Tudor screen and some fine stained glass. You'll need to make an appointment to get in - call *0207 405 8164*.

In the middle of The Strand is Temple Bar, marking the boundary between Westminster and the City of London. In medieval times this was where the heads of executed traitors were displayed.

Across the street is **Temple**, which actually comprises two Inns of Court, **Middle and Inner Temple**. A walk down Inner Temple Lane will bring you to **Temple Church**, built in 1185, one of the oldest surviving buildings in London. It was built by the Knights Templar, whose job was to protect pilgrims on the way to Jerusalem. The church, which is basically round, is a real gem, with lots of disgruntled-looking statues and effigies. Maybe that's not so surprising: The knights, who started off poor and strapped for cash, got rich as wealthy pilgrims showered them with gifts; by the 14th century, they were being accused of all manner of dastardly behavior, including sodomy and blasphemy. So they were thrown into the Tower and stripped of their wealth. Meanwhile, individual naughty knights were locked away in a tiny five foot cell at the north western corner of the choir. You can still see it today. *(Open Wednesday to Sunday 10am to 4pm. Closed August)*

Middle Temple Hall *(Open during term time Monday to Friday 10am to noon and 3pm to 4.30pm)* was the place where medieval law students were accommodated, as well as the place where they attended lectures. It also doubled up as an entertainment venue: Elizabethan masques and plays were put on here, and the first production of Master Shakespeare's *Twelfth Night* was performed here in 1602. The Hall is notable for its woodwork; a fine hammerbeam roof and paneling, and for the portraits of Tudor monarchs.

Prince Henry's Room
17 Fleet Street, EC4
Tel. 0207 936 2710
Open Monday to Saturday 11am to 2pm
Admission: Free
Nearest Tube: Temple

The name of this 1610 half-timbered house is misleading. Prince Henry, James I's popular eldest son, did not live or even stay here. Rather, there's always been an inn here called *The Prince's Arms*, and when Prince Henry was invested as Prince of Wales, the first-floor room was dedicated in his honor. It's marked with his coat of arms and you can see the letters 'PH' on the original lime plaster ceiling. See the superb Jacobean oak paneling and some stained glass windows installed to commemorate the building's rescue from demolition in 1906. There's a small exhibition dedicated to the life and work of **Samuel Pepys**. Technically in The City, this attraction has been included here for convenience.

Hunterian Museum
35-43 Lincoln's Inn Fields, WC2
Tel 0207 869 6560
www.rcseng.ac.uk/services/museums
Call to check opening times and admission prices
Nearest Tube: Holborn

Founded in 1813, this museum closed temporarily in 2002 and was due to open again in early 2005. Bizarre, but strangely compelling, you can see a mummified hand,

THEATRE

Theatre tickets are available at **agencies** all over the city, but it may work out cheaper for you if you're able to book your tickets before leaving home. At **Leicester Square ticket booth** you can buy last-minute, same-day tickets at half prices.

The Official London Theatre Guide produces a comprehensive, up-to-date theater guide regularly throughout the year. You can access this online (*www.OfficialLondonTheatre.co.uk*) or you can contact one of the major ticket agencies direct, like **Ticketmaster** *(Tel. 0207 413 1442, www.ticketmaster.co.uk* or **First call** *(Tel. 0207 497 9977)*. Have your credit card handy.

Most of London's theaters are small – around 500 seats – and laid out in tiers with the stalls occupying the main floor and various circles above. Playbills are called programs and are available before the performance and during the interval (intermission). Many theaters have bars open before a performance where you can also order your drinks for the interval, avoiding long queues. (See Walks)

early wax models of dissections, a row of foetal skeletons, ranging from a child of three months through to the skeleton of the 'Irish Giant', well over seven feet tall. To be honest, an hour or so spent here makes a visit to the Chamber of Horrors seem like a family picnic.

Sir John Soane's Museum
13 Lincoln's Inn Fields, WC2
Tel. 0207 405 2107
www.soane.org
Open year-round Tuesday to Saturday 10am to 5pm (1ˢᵗ Tuesday of the month to 9pm)
Admission: free. Tours (Saturday, 2.30pm): £3
Nearest Tube: Holborn

This fascinating property is virtually unchanged from the days when it was the home of Soane, a leading architect in the late 18th and early 19th centuries. See the original of Hogarth's *The Rake's Progress* in the **Picture Room**, the **Dining Room** with its unusual use of mirrors, and the **Monk's Parlour and Cloister**, a bizarre Gothic folly dedicated to a make-believe friar, complete with tomb, and medieval casts, gargoyles and a model of an Etruscan tomb containing a skeleton! The house is brimming with other, equally intriguing (or mortifying, in some cases) artifacts and antiquities – including some of Soane's 30,000-strong collection of drawings.

Dickens' House
48 Doughty Street, WC1
Tel. 0207 405 2127
www.dickensmuseum.com
Open Monday to Saturday, 10am to 5pm
Admission: £4
Nearest Tube: Russell Square

This four-storey townhouse in Bloomsbury is the only survivor of Dickens' several London residences. He penned *Nicholas Nickelby*, *The Pickwick Papers* and *Oliver Twist* during a two-year (1837-1839) sojourn here. The place is full of drawings, paintings – including a miniature of Dickens painted by his aunt in 1830 - manuscripts and personal effects, including quill pens and some of the desks he used during his career. It's a real insight not only into Dickens himself, but into Victorian London that the author so loved – and despised. For all you Lionel Bart fans, there's even an original score for the blockbuster musical *Oliver!*

Coram Foundation
40 Brunswick Square, WC1
Tel. 0207 841 3600
www.coram.org.uk
Open Tues - Sat 10am - 6pm, Sun 12noon - 6pm
Admission £5
Nearest Tube: Russell Square

Thomas Coram was an 18th century sea captain from Lyme Regis in Dorset who made his fortune trading between the Old World and the New. Deeply moved by the plight of London's children, many abandoned or living life on the streets, he set about raising the money to build his '**Foundling Hospital**'. His friend, the composer Handel, donated an organ to the cause and the painter Hogarth became one of the hospital governors. Even the king himself got involved. The hospital moved out to Hertfordshire in the 1920s, but the buildings remain and now house an intriguing **Museum**. You'll find works of art by Hogarth and Gainsborough, original scores by Handel, and a history of the Foundation's development.

The British Museum
Great Russell Street, WC1
Tel 0207 636 1555
www.thebritishmuseum.ac.uk
Open Monday to Saturday 10am to 5pm, Sunday noon to 6pm
Admission free

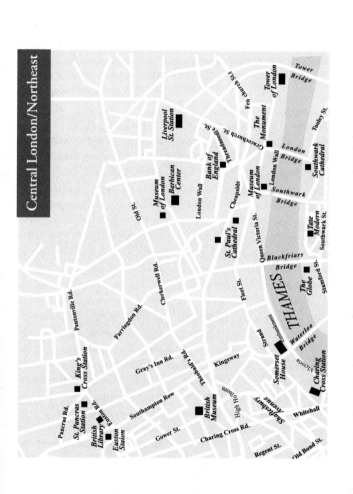

Central London/Northeast

Nearest Tube: Holborn, Tottenham Court Road

The mind-blowing British Museum contains one of the most extensive collections of art and artifacts in the world. There are world-famous collections of **antiquities** from Egypt, Western Asia, Greece and Rome, as well as Prehistoric and Romano-British, Medieval Renaissance, Modern and Oriental collections; prints and drawing – some six and a half million items, ranging from fragments of ancient manuscripts to colossal statues and all spread out over 13 acres. Although it may sound overwhelming, the great thing about this vast collection is that it's so well laid out that you can easily call it quits one day and resume your tour another.

As you enter the front hall, check out the **Assyrian Transept**. Here, the winged and human-headed bulls and lions that once guarded the gateways to the palaces of Assyrian kings. Nearby is the **Black Obelisk of Shalmaneser III**, depicting Jehu, King of Israel, paying tribute. From here you can access the hall of Egyptian sculpture and see the famous **Rosetta Stone**, whose discovery paved the way to the decoding of hyrogliphics. Also on the ground floor is the **Duveen Gallery**, where you'll find the renowned **Elgin Marbles** – still the cause of much friction between Britain and Greece, which desires their return – are kept.

Also on the ground floor is the **Manuscripts Room**, with an amazing range of manuscripts of every kind – Dickens' hand-written draft of *Nicholas Nickelby*, the original manuscripts of several Beatles' songs, Handel's *Messiah*, an original **Magna Carta**, a 15th century edition of Chaucer's *Canterbury Tales* and the famous **Gutenburg Bible** of 1455.

On the second floor are the galleries of the Department of **Medieval and Later Antiquities**. One of the most interesting exhibits here is the remains of an **Anglo-Saxon burial ship**, discovered at Sutton Hoo in Suffolk, containing gold jewelry, armor, weapons, silverware and other implements.

The main attractions of the **upper floor** are the **Egyptian Antiquities**, the largest and most comprehensive collection outside Cairo. **Room 63** is magnificent, looking like a set from *The Mummy*. The collection illustrates every aspect of ancient Egyptian culture from pre-dynastic times (c4000BC) to the Coptic period (12th century AD) including a large amount of material from Nubia and the Sudan. The recently-installed Japanese galleries on the top floor are softly-lit, uncrowded and well worth a visit.

If you need a break, there's a pleasant **cafe** on the ground floor, just past the bookshop, where you can get tea, coffee and sandwiches. For something more substantial, try the **restaurant**, which serves hot meals from about a fiver.

Trafalgar Square, Piccadilly, & Soho

Trafalgar Square
Trafalgar Square, WC2
Nearest Tube: Charing Cross

London's most famous square was built on the site of the **Royal Mews**, where Edward I kept his royal hawks. Today it's the point from which all distances to and from the capital are measured. Flanked on its northern side by the **National Gallery**, and overlooked by the graceful spire of **St Martin-in-the-Fields**, its centerpiece is the 17 foot statue of **Lord Nelson**, perched on column 145 feet high. The fountains and the four lions around the base were added in 1867. The square is notorious for the thousands of pigeons that descend upon it daily; after 150 years of encrustation with pigeon poo, Lord Nelson himself is now protected with a pigeon-proof gel coating.

Unless you happen to be smeared with a similar concoction yourself, then beware! You have been warned!

RESTAURANT TIPS
New World
1 Gerrard Place, W1
Tel. 0207 734 0677
Nearest Tube:
Leicester Square

Dim Sum is one of London's cheapest epicurean thrills; two hungry people would have difficulty spending more than £20 between them. Though it seats 500, it can get packed, especially lunchtimes.

China China
3 Gerrard Street, W1
Tel. 0207 439 7502
Nearest Tube:
Leicester Square

This four-story Chinese restaurant stays open late, and the service is pretty good (though a smile wouldn't hurt here and there). Best of all, the Cantonese food is excellent and there are always lots of Chinese eating here – always a good sign. ✳

The National Gallery
Trafalgar Square, WC2
Tel. 0207 839 2885
www.nationalgallery.org.uk
Open daily 10am to 6pm
Admission: free
Nearest Tube: Charing Cross

Occupying one side of Trafalgar Square, the neo-classical National Gallery houses one of the most comprehensive collections of **western paintings** in the world. Given the number of works on display, it's remarkably uncluttered.

The collection spans the history of art from the 13th to the 20th century. Among the earliest works, the **Wilton Diptych** (French School, late 14th century) is the greatest treasure. It shows Richard II being introduced to the Madonna and Child by John the Baptist and Saxon King Edward the Confessor (founder of Westminster Abbey).

Italian art, much of which you'll find in the **Sainsbury Wing**, is represented by Masaccio, della Francesca, da Vinci, Michelangelo, a roomful of Raphaels, with the breathtaking *Crucifixion* as a centerpiece, and notable works by Titian, Tintoretto and Veronese. Northern European painters are well represented; Breughel's *Adoration*, Vermeer's *Young Woman at a Virginal* and de Hooch's *Patio in a in Delft* are three of the most memorable.

Check out a roomful of Rembrandts, including four stunning portraits, a roomful of Rubens, Van Dyke's massive and famous painting of an equestrian Charles I, as well as works by some of the greatest **British** artists – Constable, Turner, Reynolds, Gainsborough and Hogarth. **Spanish** art is represented by Velesquez, El Greco, and Goya, while other rooms are dedicated to **French** painters, such as Delacroix and Ingres, 19th century impressionists like Manet, Monet and Renoir, and postimpressionists like Cezanne and Van Gogh.

If you're needing refreshment here, the **Brasserie** restaurant on the first floor of the Sainsbury Wing has an Italian-style **coffee bar**, which includes sandwiches and salads and more exotic fare (Lincolnshire sausages, grilled vegetables etc) at lunchtimes.

This neighborhood pub behind Charing Cross Station was a frequent haunt of Sir Arthur Conan Doyle and features in his most famous tome, *The Hound of the Baskervilles.* Tourists are inevitably drawn by the literary association, and the various Holmes memorabilia scattered about the place. ❋

St. Martin-in-the-Fields
*Trafalgar Square, WC2
Tel. 0207 766 1199
www.stmartin-in-the-fields.org
Open daily 8am to 6.30pm
Admission: free
Nearest Tube: Charing Cross*

Probably London's most famous church after St Paul's Cathedral and Westminster Abbey, St Martin's was built in 1726 by architect James Gibbs, whose classic design was the inspiration for countless colonial churches across

Located alongside the famous church, this market has about 200 stalls loaded with real bargains: ceramics, jewelry, fine art, clothes and textiles.

Charing Cross
Collectors' Fair
*Villiers Street, WC2
Tel. 0208 398 8065
Nearest Tube:
Charing Cross
Open Saturdays only
8.30am to 5pm*

Small, popular antiques and flea market with everything from furniture accessories to stamps, coins and medals. Small eccentric items make it a great place to shop for unusual gifts. ❋

the Pond. The church is popular with music lovers – the **Academy of St Martin-in-the-Fields** is rooted here – and concerts take place regularly. The church has a fine reputation for caring for London's homeless, work that is partly funded by the excellent **restaurant** in the crypt. Here also is the **London Brass Rubbing Centre**, where all the bits and pieces needed to make your own souvenir knight from replica tomb brasses.

The National Portrait Gallery
2, St Martin's Place, WC2
Tel. 0207 312 2463
www.npg.org.uk
Open Monday to Saturday 10am to 6pm, Sunday noon to 6pm.
Admission free
Nearest Tube: Leicester Square

Many of the most famous faces from English history can be found at the National Portrait Gallery, just behind the National Gallery, off Trafalgar Square. Gaze into the lecherous eyes of **Henry VIII**, exchange doleful looks with **D.H Lawrence**, and try to make **Queen Victoria** giggle. Most of the portraits are by famous artists, such as Sir Joshua Reynolds, or Holbein right through to Andy Warhol. There's a wonderful painting of **Sir Winston Churchill** by Walter Sickert, and a famous George Beresford photograph of **Virginia Woolf**.

On the next landing, you'll find a roomful of portraits of the current royal family, including several of the Queen, one of which, reportedly, particularly upset her.

ENTERTAINMENT TIP

Check *Time Out* or one of the other listings magazines for more what's playing where. The big venues are **The Barbican Centre**, *Tel. 0207 638 8891*, housing the Royal Shakespeare Company and the London Symphony; the **English National Opera**, *Tel. 0207 632 8300*; the **Royal Opera House**, Covent Garden, *Tel. 0207 240 1066*, routinely featuring the greatest names in the opera world; and the **Royal Albert Hall**, *Tel. 0207 589 8212*, with pop and classical concerts. From the end of the summer into November, the world's greatest musical festival is staged here – the famous Promenade Concerts. ✤

Then on the next floor, there's Boldini's portrait of **Lady Colin Campbell**, a Rodin bust and a portrait of the **Bronte sisters** painted by their artist brother Brangwen. On level four, a roomful of **English kings** is on display, all painted in the 16th century on board in the style of Holbein, while on level 5, there are some wonderful Gainsboroughs and Reynolds.

Piccadilly Circus
Piccadilly Circus, WC2
Nearest Tube: Piccadilly Circus

The junction of five major roads, Piccadilly Circus, with its famous statue (not of Eros, as frequently surmised, but of **'The Angel of Christian Charity'**), takes its name from Piccadilly Hall, a long gone mansion that was built in the 17th century by a local tailor from the proceeds of the sale of picadils – a type of rough (collar) that was very popular at the time. The statue, usually hidden behind a sea of backpackers, was commissioned in 1893 as a memorial to the great philanthropist Lord Shaftesbury. Made (unusually for its time) of aluminum, it cost £7,000 – though the sculptor Albert Gilbert was only paid £3,000 and immediately became bankrupt. The

much-photographed northern side of the Circus is flanked by some rather ordinary-looking buildings covered by a layer of neon advertisements.

Leicester Square
Leicester Square, WC2
Nearest Tube: Leicester Square

You'd never think that this square was originally laid out in the 1630s, as so many of the facades have given way to vast advertising hoardings and acres of neon lights. This is the focal point of West End nightlife, with several cinemas, dozens of restaurants and a

SHOPPING TIPS
Burberry's
161-165 Regent Street, W1
Nearest Tube: Piccadilly Circus

Famous for its raincoats, a must-have if you're spending any length of time in London.

Herbert Johnson
30 New Bond Street, W1
Nearest Tube: Bond Street

Old-world gentleman's hatter, still producing deerstalkers, bowlers, flatcaps and panamas. ❉

handful of theaters within a stone's throw.

Royal Academy of Arts
Burlington House, Piccadilly, W1
Tel. 0207 300 8000
www.royalacademy.org.uk

Open Monday to Thursday and Saturday to Sunday 10am to 6pm, Friday 10am to 8.30pm. Admission: prices vary, depending on exhibition.
Nearest Tube: Green Park

The Royal Academy – whose members include just about all the members of the British art and architectural establishment – has been housed in **Burlington House**, an elegant Palladian mansion built for the Earl of Burlington, since 1837. The collection includes works by just about every member – Gainsborough, Turner and Constable, for example – but the *piece de resistance* must be a sculpted disc of the *Madonna and Child* by Michelangelo, in the **Sackler Galleries**. The Academy is well known for its oopular **Summer Exhibition**, a hotch-potch of up to 1,000 items of sculpture and paintings. More serious, superbly-organised exhibitions are held throughout the year. There's a very good **café**, and one of the best **museum shops** in London.

Oxford Street to King's Cross

Oxford Street
London's prime retail drag is a two-mile stretch of large department stores, high street clothing outlets, banks, bookstores and cafes. The crowds here are enormous, particularly on Saturdays and in the run-up to Christmas, when the area should be avoided at all costs.

Wallace Collection
Hertford House, Manchester Square, W1
Tel. 0207 935 9500
www.wallace-collction.com
Open Monday to Saturday 10am to 5pm, Sunday noon to 5pm
Admission: free
Nearest Tube: Bond Street

One of the best small galleries in London, the Wallace contains exquisite pieces of art mainly from the 17th and 18th centuries, housed in a ravishing **Italianate mansion**, that's worth a visit in its own right. The collection, brought together by four generations of Marquesses of Hertford, contains works by Titian, Rubens and Rembrandt, with a fine portrait of his son on display. The **French Rooms** contain works that were purchased for peanuts after the French Revolution rendered them out of fashion. Some exquisite furniture and sculptures complement the paintings. In the basement, four new galleries are devoted to watercolors and conservation.

Speaker's Corner
Marble Arch, W1
Nearest Tube: Marble Arch

Every Sunday afternoon hundreds of people descend on the north east corner of Hyde Park, when anyone – yourself included - is allowed to mount a soapbox and say their piece, on any subject from the war against terror to the price of underwear in Madagascar. Of more interest, perhaps, is nearby **Marble Arch**, built in 1827 near Buckingham Palace, moved here in 1851. On the sidewalk by the arch is a plaque making the spot where the 'Tyburn Tree' – London's main gallows – stood until 1783. The wooden construction could stage 21 hangings at a time, and drew huge crowds to watch the spectacle.

SHOPPING TIP
La Fromagerie
2-4 Moxon Street, W1
Tel. 0207 935 0341
Nearest Tube:
Baker Street

A must for cheese lovers, La Fromagerie is dedicated to the sale of fine cheeses from France, Britain, Italy and beyond. You can also load up on fine wines, hand baked breads and cured meats. Guaranteed to make you drool! ✤

Handel House Museum
23-25 Brook Street, W1
Tel. 0207 495 1685
www.handelhouse.org
Open Tuesday, Wednesday, Friday and Saturday 10am to 6pm; Thursday 10am to 8pm, Sunday noon to 6pm
Admission: £4.50
Nearest Tube: Bond Street

The composer of *Water Music* lived at 25 Brook Street from 1723 until his death in 1759. The museum, London's first to be dedicated to a composer, brims with personal effects, pictures and music manuscripts.

Sherlock Holmes Museum
221b Baker Street, NW1
Tel. 0207 935 8866
www.sherlock-holmes.co.uk
Open daily 9.30am to 6pm
Admission: £6
Nearest Tube: Baker Street

The museum consists of a three-floor reconstruction of Holmes' famous apartment, all based on details primed from the Conan Doyle books. With life-size wax models of Holmes characters, authentic period furniture and fittings, and assorted Holmes memorabilia, this museum is elementary for all fans of the great detective.

SHOPPING TIPS
Selfridge's
400 Oxford Street, W1, Tel. 0870 837 7377,
www.selfridges.com. Nearest Tube: Marble Arch

Not quite as big as Harrods, but almost as famous, this imposing and recently refurbished stately Edwardian store dominates the western end of Oxford Street. It's renowned for its designer fashion and for an excellent food hall.

Marks and Spencer
458 Oxford Street, W1, Tel. 0207 935 7954,
www.marksandspencer.co.uk. Nearest Tube: Marble Arch

Despite poor sales figures in recent years, the nationwide chain's flagship store at Marble Arch is still the busiest retail store (per square foot) in the world. Marks and Sparks, as it's known, is famed for sturdy, practical clothes and for the food departments with an abundance of very high quality prepared meals. There's scarcely a Brit alive who hasn't bought his/her underwear here.

Thomas Goode
19 South Audley Street, W1, Tel. 0207 499 2823,
www.thomasgoode.co.uk. Nearest Tube: Green Park or
Bond Street

The best formal china and leaded crystal.

English Teddy Bear Company
153 Regent Street, W1, Tel. 0207 287 3273
Nearest Tube: Oxford Circus

Fine hand-crafted teddy bears, a l'anglais. Look out for their limited editions.

Hope and Glory
131a Kensington Church Street, W8, Tel. 0207 727
8424. Nearest Tube: Notting Hill Gate

Specializes in commemorative glass and china from 1887 onwards.

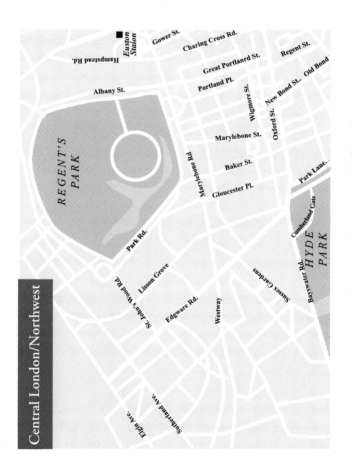

Central London/Northwest

Madame Tussaud's
Marylebone Road, NW1
Tel. 0207 400 3000
www.madame-tussauds.com
*Open Monday to Friday 10am
to 5.30pm, Saturday and Sunday from 9.30am*
Admission, adults £9.50, children £6.25, under 5 free
Nearest Tube: Baker Street

See the Queen again at Madame Tussaud's waxworks, on Marylebone Road. Tussaud's owes its existence to a certain **Dr Curtius**, who in 1770 opened an exhibition of life-size wax models in Paris. His niece, Marie Tussaud, learned the secret of making lifelike replicas of famous people, and so Madame Tussaud's was born.

Some of the older figures on display come from molds taken by Madame Tussaud herself, but most of the models are much more recent. They include effigies of kings and queen through the ages, past and current world leaders, and of course rock, pop and sports stars – a real who's who.

Most popular, especially with younger visitors, is the **Chamber of Horrors**, where some of the world's most grisly murder and torture scenes

have been reconstructed; there's even a Victorian London Street with a figure of Jack the Ripper lurking in the shadows!

New technologies have been adopted to bring some of the models "to life," there's a garden party where you can mix with the rich and famous, and a new attraction which explores Madame Tussaud's 200 year history.

London Zoo
Regent's Park, NW1
Tel. 0207 722 3333
www.londonzoo.co.uk
Open daily 10am to 5.30pm
Admission: £9
Nearest Tube: Regent's Park

This well-kept Zoo, in a corner of **Regent's Park**, was established in 1828, its nucleus a collection of gifts to the royal family: a hippo, two giraffes, a chimp and a number of thylacines, sadly now extinct. The zoo's collection has expanded greatly since, and along with all the expected residents you can see an anoa, a pudu, a leadbetter's possum, a bird-eating spider and a herd of oyrx. The excellent reptile house is just as frightening as any Chamber of Horrors! There's a Children's Zoo with goats, sheep, ponies and rabbits for petting, plus a selection of cafes and restaurants serving hot and cold food at reasonable prices.

British Library
96 Euston Road, NW1
Tel. 0207 412 7000
www.bl.uk
Open Monday 9.30am to 6pm, Tuesday 9.30am to 8pm, Wednesday to Friday 9.30am to 6pm, Saturday 9.30am to 5pm, Sunday 11am to 5pm
Admission: free
Nearest Tube: King's Cross

One of the Britain's best contemporary public buildings for years, the new British Library was completed in 1998 and stands in a piazza off the Euston Road, an amazing contrast to the heavy Gothic **St Pancras Station** which seems to frown at its modern design. The Library stocks all British publications in print and a wealth of historical manuscripts, books and maps in its exhibition galleries, ranging from an original Magna Carta and a Gutenburg Bible to original Beatles' scores. It also houses a fine collection of paintings, sculptures and tapestries by living British artists.

King's Cross Station
Euston Road, NW1
Nearest Tube: King's Cross

London's main train terminus for the east coast (Newcastle and Edinburgh) line is a striking piece of architecture in its own right but is probably better known today for its association with a young wizard. Harry Potter walks into a wall onto platform 9 3/4 to catch the Hogwarts Express before it puffs its way to the legendary school. Don't attempt to do it yourself.

The City and East End

Dr. Johnson's House
17 Gough Square, EC4
Tel. 0207 353 3745
www.drjh.dircon.co.uk
Open May to September, Monday to Saturday 11am to 5.30pm; rest of year closes at 5pm

Admission £4
Nearest Tube: Blackfriars

This rather fetching Georgian town house where the famous lexicographer – best known for his dictionary published in 1755 – resided from 1748 to 1759. There are portraits of Johnson and his contemporaries, including one of his black servant, Francis Barber, as well as a first edition of the dictionary, a coffee cup that belonged to his friend and biographer Dr Boswell, and Johnson's gout chair from the nearby Cock Tavern, his favorite 'local'.

SHOPPING TIP
London Silver Vaults
53-64 Chancery Lane, WC2
Tel. 0207 242 3844
www.thesilvervaults.com
Open Monday to Friday 9am to 5.30pm, Saturday 9am to 1pm
Nearest Tube: Chancery Lane

Hidden away behind large safe doors, the vaults house dozens of specialist dealers, purveying everything from the finest jewelry to cutlery. ❁

St. Bride's Church
Fleet Street, EC4
Tel. 0207 353 1301
Open daily 8am to 4.45pm
Admission: free
Nearest Tube: Blackfriars

Christopher Wren built this small but beautiful church in 1671, after an earlier building was destroyed in the Great Fire of 1665. It's known as the **journalists' church** on account of its Fleet Street location. Note the elegant steeple, which was the inspiration for the white, tiered wedding cake design. There's a small but fascinating exhibit of nearby excavated artifacts – including some roman coins – in the crypt.

St. Paul's Cathedral
St Paul's Churchyard, EC4
Tel 0207 236 4128
www.stpauls.co.uk
Open Monday to Saturday 8.30am to 4pm
Admission free, but charge to crypt: adults £4, children £2
Nearest Tube: St Paul's

Completed in 1710 and replacing an even bigger medieval cathedral, St Paul's still manages to dominate the City skyline, despite the encroachment of Sir Basil Spence's 'Gherkin' and other city skyscrapers. When **Old St Paul's** was ravaged by the **Great Fire of London**, tenders were put out for a new cathedral to replace it. The new cathedral's radically different design was provided by **Sir Christopher Wren**, whose new Renaissance style structure stretches just over 500ft in length and

PUB TIPS

The Black Friar
174 Queen Victoria Street, EC4
Tel 0207 236 5650
Nearest Tube:
Blackfriars

This amazing art nouveau pub is a real gem. Located on the site of a former Dominican monastery, the Black Friar's decor – inlaid mother-of-pearl, gold mosaic ceilings, bronze reliefs of monks etc. – make it worth a visit for the architecture alone.

Ye Olde Cheshire Cheese
145 Fleet Street, EC4
Tel 0207 353 6170
Nearest Tube: Holborn

Dating from 1667, and built over the earlier remains of Whitefriars' monastery, this ia real charmer, with sawdust-sprinkled floors, beamed ceilings, working fireplaces and dark wood paneling throughout. Samuel Johnson, Oliver Goldsmith and Charles Dickens were regulars.
❀

365ft from ground level to the top of the dome – a fitting scene for the royal wedding of Prince Charles to Lady Diana Spencer in 1981.

St Paul's classical **dome** dominates the building. You can climb to the level of the **Whispering Gallery** (so-called because a visitor whispering into the wall on one side can be heard by another on the other side), and higher still, to the **Stone Gallery**, for a spectacular 360 degree view of London.

The cathedral is made out in the shape of a Latin cross. It contains surprisingly few art treasures – (**Grinling Gibbons'** beautifully carved choir stalls being an exception) but there are a host of **monuments**, including one to the **Duke of Wellington**, and a **memorial chapel** to the **American servicemen and women** who lost their lives while stationed in the UK during WWII.

Below the nave, the crypt contains tombs and monuments to statesmen and military leaders such as **Nelson**, and there's a fascinating scale model of the old cathedral, with its 500ft spire.

One of highlights of this, and

of many other English cathedrals, is the opportunity to listen to the **choir**. The service of Evensong is performed here daily at 5pm on weekdays and 3.15pm Sundays, by the men and boy choir of St Paul's - one of the best.

RESTAURANT TIP
Le Poulbot
45 Cheapside, EC2
Tel. 0207 236 4379
Nearest Tube: St Paul's
Lunch only

A Roux-brothers' gem, and a favorite haunt of city gents, though the French-style food is a bit more pricey than the address suggests. ❋

Priory Church of
St. Bartholomew the Great
Bartholomew Close (off Little Britain), EC1
Tel. 0207 606 5171
www.greatstbarts.com
Open Tuesday to Friday 8.30am to 5pm (4 p.m. from mid-November to mid-February) Saturday 10.30am to 1.30pm Sunday 8.30am to 1.00pm and 2.30pm to 8.00pm
Admission: free
Nearest Tube: St Paul's

This gem of a church is one of London's oldest. It dates from 1123, when it was founded by Henry I's court jester, **Rahere**, the brains behind St Bartholomew's Hospital, opposite. Although a later Henry (VIII) did his best to destroy the church during the Dissolution of the Monasteries, and to some degree succeeded, much of the original **Norman choir** survives. It also survived the Great Fire of London, when the wind suddenly changed direction. Over the years it has been used as a blacksmith's, a stable and a printing works (Benjamin Franklin worked here for a while). Today, it's an amazingly peaceful oasis of calm and tranquillity in one of London's busiest neighborhoods.

SHOPPING TIP
Smiths of Smithfields
67 Charterhouse Street, EC1
Tel. 0207 236 6666
www.smithsofsmithfield.co.uk
Nearest Tube: St Paul's

This renovated, former meat packing warehouse overlooking London's central meat market has several floors of yummy food, drink and culture. Not to be missed. ❋

St. John's Gate
St. John's Lane, EC1
Tel. 0207 253 6644
www.sja.org.uk
Open Friday 10am to 5pm,
Saturday 10am to 4pm
Admission free. Tours (Tues-
day, Friday and Saturday at
11am and 2.30pm): £4
Nearest Tube: Farringdon

Given the ferocity of the Great Fire of London you'd be forgiven for thinking that nothing at all survived. But this early 16th century gate did, although heavily restored 300 years later. Inside there's a small but interesting museum all about the **Order of St John**, an ancient community of knights who provided nursing care during the Crusades.

The Museum of London
150 London Wall, near Barbican Centre
Tel 020 7730 0717
www.museumoflondon.org.uk
Open Monday to Saturday 10am to 5.50pm, Sunday noon to 5.50pm
Admission adults £5, children £3
Nearest Tube: Barbican

This modern concrete and glass building traces the history of London from the Ice Age through to the present in a combination of ancient antiquities, costume, furniture, war posters, ration books and all kinds of memorabilia.

While the Ice Age exhibition is a must for kids, it's best to breeze through here to **Roman London**, where you can see a mammoth tooth found near Downing Street, a chopping tool found near the Bloomsbury YMCA and a pair of bone tweezers, and an new addition – a reconstruction of a London street in Roman times, complete with sounds – and smells! You'll find a reconstructed Roman kitchen, dining room and dressing table with elaborate jewelry and cosmetics from the period. Further on, a **Viking** battle ax is a reminder of a 9th century invasion of London by 300 Viking ships.

Other displays include the construction of the original **London Bridge** in about 1200, maps of medieval England, the building of a **Tudor house**, **Oliver Cromwell's** death mask, and the original **Mortality Broadsheet** listing the names of all the London plague deaths between November 1602 and November 1603 – 37,000 in all. There's a display about the **Great Fire of London** in 1666, with a narration from Samuel Pepys' diary.

You can also see the Lord Mayor of London's coach, still used once a year on Lord Mayor's Day, and an 1890 hansom cab, an art deco elevator from Selfridge's store on Oxford Street, and a reconstructed 19th century High Street. There's a large costume department where the stars are Roman vestments and a 19th century dandy's outfit.

Clockmakers' Collection
The Guildhall, EC1
Tel 0207 606 3030
www.clockmakers.org
Open Monday to Friday 9.30am to 4.30pm
Admission: Free
Nearest Tube: Bank

Housed on permanent display in the **Guildhall Library**, The Clockmakers' Collection was begun in 1814, the oldest collection specifically of clocks and watches in the world. The timepieces are on display in a single room, containing at any one time some 600 English and European watches, 30 clocks and 15 marine timekeepers. Look out for the skull-faced watch that once belonged to Mary, Queen of Scots.

Bank of England Museum
Bartholomew Lane, EC2
Tel. 0207 641 5555
www.bankofengland.co.uk/museum
Open Monday to Friday 10am to 5pm
Admission: free
Nearest Tube: Bank.

Even if you're not really interested in financial matters, this fairly new (1988) museum is bound to grab your attention with its comprehensive history of the 'Old Lady of Threadneedle Street' and of banking in general.

SHOPPING TIP
Leadenhall Market
Whittington Avenue, EC3
Nearest Tube: Monument

Restored Victorian food market where you can pick up gourmet food at a fraction of what you'd pay in a supermarket. Cheese, seafood, meat and poultry and game are all here in abundance. What with the glass roof and cobbled alleyways, and general hubbub, it's about as close as you can get to the atmosphere of Victorian London.

The Monument
Monument Street, EC3
Tel. 0207 626 2717
Open daily 10am to 5.30pm.
Admission: £1.50
Nearest Tube: Bank

This strange looking column topped by a golden ball is the work of Sir Christopher Wren. Built to commemorate the Great Fire of London, it is close to the spot in **Pudding Lane** where the Fire is alleged to have started. You can walk up the 311 steps to a viewing platform.

Bevis Marks Synagogue
Bevis Marks, EC3
Tel. 0207 626 1274
Open Sunday 11am- 12.30pm,
Monday to Wednesday, 11.30am-
1pm, Friday, 11.30am-1pm
(Summertime only)

First opened in 1701, this is the oldest synagogue still in use in Britain. Jews first arrived in England in 1066 with William the Conqueror, but were expelled from the country in 1290. For more than 350 years there were no Jewish communities or places of worship in Britain. Then in the early 17th century a number of Jews, fleeing the Inquisition, arrived to settle in the City of London – though they were still forbidden to practise their religion in public.

In 1655 a group of them petitioned Oliver Cromwell for permission to worship and to re-admit Jews to England. Cromwell gave tacit approval

RESTAURANT TIPS
Prism
147 Leadenhall Street,
EC3
Tel. 0207 256 3888
Closed weekends
Nearest Tube: Bank

Former banking hall with high ceilings and lofty pillars that's been transformed into one of the City's most beguiling restaurants with a menu that includes traditional English favorites, with a modern twist.

The Poet
20 Creechurch Lane,
EC3
Tel. 0207 623 3999
Closed weekends
Nearest Tube: Bank

The place positively buzzes, especially at lunchtime. For the best value, try the brasserie downstairs with its glorified bar snacks. ❧

and in 1656 the upper floor of a house in nearby Creechurch Lane was opened for use as a place of worship. Construction of a new synagogue began in 1699 built by Joseph Avis, a Quaker. It was finished in 1701 at a cost of £2,650. It is believed that Princess (later Queen) Anne presented an oak beam from a Royal Navy ship for use as a roof support for the Synagogue building. The building was badly damaged by the terrorist bombs which hit the City of London in 1992 and 1993. Since then it has been repaired and renovated so that today it appears much as it did on its opening day in 1701.

The Tower of London
Tower Hill, EC3
Tel. 0207 709 0765
www.hrp.org.uk
Open Monday to Saturday 9am to 6pm, Sunday 10am to 6pm
Admission: £11.30
Nearest Tube: Tower Hill

London's top visitor attraction is best known for its gory associations with many of the nation's most famous historical figures - **Anne Boleyn** and **Sir Thomas More** to name just a couple – and for the famous **"Beefeaters"** or yeomen of the guard – honorary members of the Queen's bodyguard, who double up as very informative and helpful tour guides.

There has been a fortress on the site since Roman times, though little of the original fortress, save a few walls, remains. **William the Conqueror**, seeking to consolidate his new power base in London, built the **White Tower** in 1078. With walls up to 15' thick and at 90ft in height, the Tower stands sentinel over the rest of the fortress. Inside, there has been a collection of armour since the time of Henry and in the basement there's an exhibition of gruesome tools used in various methods of torture. A more reflective atmosphere pervades in the **Chapel of St John**, on the second floor, pure and simple Norman in style. Close to the White Tower is another spiritual oasis; the **Chapel of St Peter ad Vincula**, now fully-restored to its Tudor glory, with fine ceiling made from Spanish chestnut, and the tombs of Anne Boleyn, Catherine Howard and Sir Thomas More, now officially a saint. The chapel can only be entered as part of an official tour.

Other must-see parts of the complex are the **Bloody Tower**, where the Little

Princes (Edward V and the Duke of York) were allegedly murdered by their uncle, Richard II, and the **Traitor's Gate**, once the Tower's main entrance from the Thames. **Tower Green**, just north of the Tower, and outside its walls, was the main **mass execution** site. Privileged prisoners, however, like Anne Boleyn and Katherine Howard, two of Henry VIII's wives, Lady Jane Grey and Sir Thomas More met their grisly end inside the Tower precincts.

There's a happier atmosphere in the **Jewel House**, the main attraction within the Tower complex, but be prepared for long lines – especially in summer. See the **Imperial State Crown**, made for Victoria's coronation in 1838. It has nearly 3,000 stones, mainly diamonds, including a priceless ruby worn by Henry V at the Battle of Agincourt in 1415. The **Second Star of Africa**, a 320-carat diamond is also stunning, but even bigger is the **First Star of Africa**, the largest cut diamond in the world. It's part of the **Sceptre with the Cross**.

If you're here at the right time, you might catch one of the Tower's ancient ceremonies – the **Ceremony of the Keys**, which goes back more than 700 years. Every night at 9.40, a sentry is challenged at the gate. His response, "Who goes there?" is followed by an identification of the keys and the presenting of arms.

Six large **ravens** are kept in the Tower and are listed as official Tower residents. They're all extremely well looked after, receiving special rations every day. They have to be: Legend says that as long as the birds remain in the Tower, the monarchy will survive. No wonder they had their wings clipped – although everyone had a scare when one was ravaged by a bull terrier. It managed to survive.

Tower Bridge

Tower Bridge, SE1
Tel. 0207 940 3985
www.towerbridge.org.uk
Open April to October 10am to 6.30pm, November to March 9.30am to 6pm
Admission: £6.25
Nearest Tube: Tower Hill

One of London's best-known landmarks, this lifting bridge, opened in 1894, with its two towers, still manages to dominate the skyline east of the Tower. Built of steel wrapped in Portland stone, it was built in the Gothic style to complement the Tower close by. The massive **bascules**, or 'arms,' rarely open these days, but in the Bridge's heydey, with lots more traffic on the Thames, they would open up to five times a day.

Take the elevator to the top of one of the 25m towers for great views across the city and Docklands area. You can trace the Bridge's development through the eyes of an animatronic construction worker, and the 'ghost' of its architect, Sir Horace Jones. An Edwardian-style music hall production tells the history of the Bridge.

PUB TIP
Dickens Inn
St Katherine's Way, E1
Tel: 0207 488 2208
Nearest Tube:
Tower Hill

Huge old pub in a waterside development, that was moved here, brick by brick. The wooden floors — sawdust, without the spit — enhance the atmosphere and there are lots of nautical odds and ends to remind you just how near The River you are. ❧

CHRISTMAS IN LONDON

Oxford Street, Regent Street and Knightsbridge become a mass of enthusiastic (or weary?) shoppers from about mid-November right up to Christmas Eve. Compensations, though, include fabulous street decorations in Regent Street, fantastic window displays and a huge Christmas tree in Trafalgar Square donated annually to Londoners as a gesture of good will by the people of Norway. If you have kids, Hamley's toy store in Regent Street is a must-see (*see* being the operative word; you may have to fight to get to the counter) – but any of the toy departments in the major department stores (Harrod's, Selfridges, etc) will do. Or you may wish to make your way to Fortnum & Masons in Piccadilly to load up on some stodgy (you either love it or loathe it) Christmas pudding. Go to a carol service at one of the city's great churches, or capture the atmosphere of a 'local.'

❧

Dennis Sever's House

18 Folgate, E1
Tel. 7247 4013
www.dennissevershouse.co.uk
Open 1ˢᵗ Sunday of the month 2pm to 5pm, 1ˢᵗ Monday noon to 2pm, every Monday evening (book in advance for a three-hour 'wander' with commentary.)
Admission: varies, depending on the tour
Nearest Tube: Liverpool Street

This terraced house in Shoreditch was bought by Dennis Sever, an American with a fascination for British history and architecture, who restored it to its 1724 glory (ie no modern plumbing or electricity) and turned it into what can only be described as a theater of domestic history.

Visitors follow an 'invisible' 18th century family around the premises. The house reeks with atmosphere (real smells included) as guests tour the rooms, each authentically decorated and crammed with period furniture and knick-knacks.

SHOPPING TIP
A Gold

42 Brushfield Street, E1
Tel. 0207 247 2487

Superb small specialist grocer and wine merchant a stone's throw of Spitalfields Market.

FAST FOOD TIP
Brick Lane Beigel Bake
159 Brick Lane, E1
Tel. 0207 729 0616
Nearest Tube:
Shoreditch

A remnant of the days when this was one of London's main Jewish neighborhoods, the Beigel Bake is a real gem. All kinds of toppings are available, and the prices are unbelievably low. �֍

Geffrye Museum

136 Kingsland Road, E2
Tel. 0207 739 9893
www.geffrye-museum.org.uk
Open Tuesday to Saturday 10am to 5pm, Sunday noon to 5pm
Admission: free
Nearest Tube: Old Street

Housed in what were originally 14 almshouses (built in 1715), this charmingly eccentric museum traces the development of English domestic interiors, each room painstakingly recreated in chronological order from the 1600s through to the present day.

PUB TIP
Prospect of Whitby
57 Wapping Wall, E1
Tel. 0207 481 1095
Nearest Tube: Wapping

Riverside tavern built in 1520, once known as the 'Devil's Tavern' on account of the riff-raff who used to booze here. Lovely river views, and a bit more respectable these days! ❀

Museum of Childhood
Cambridge Heath Road, E2
Tel. 0200208 980 2415
www.museumofchildhood.org.uk
Open Saturday to Thursday 10am to 5.30pm
Admission: free
Nearest Tube: Bethnal Green

This entertaining museum was the original Victoria and Albert Museum. Its original iron frame, still visible inside, was bought to Bethnal Green in the 1860s, re-erected, and finished with its distinctive red brick to the designs of J W Wild. The outside was decorated with murals depicting the arts, sciences and agriculture by F W Moody, and the marble mosaic floor was put together by women prisoners from Woking gaol.

In the 1920s, the Museum started to focus on children. One of the galleries was dedicated to childhood, childhood material was actively collected, and objects transferred from the V&A.

Finally, in 1974, it became a Museum of Childhood. Its fascinating exhibits include some very old dolls, dolls' houses (including some 18th century Baby Houses that were made not for children, but for young aristocratic women), train sets, toy cars, puppets and examples of children's clothing through the years. It's a bit of a trek from central London, but well worth the trip, especially if you have kids in tow.

Ragged School Museum
46-50 Copperfield Road, E3
Tel. 0208 980 6405
www.raggedschoolmuseum.org.uk
Open: Wednesday and Thursday 10am to 5pm
Admission: free
Nearest Tube: Stepney Green or Mile End

The Museum was opened in 1990 in three canalside warehouses in Copperfield Road, East London. These buildings were previously used by Dr Barnardo to house the largest ragged school in London. In a re-created classroom of the period, visitors can now experience how Victorian children were taught. There are also displays on local history, industry and life in the East End and a varied programme of temporary exhibitions. The Museum runs a variety of different activities for all ages. These include workshops, history talks, treasure hunts and canal walks.

Sutton House
2 and 4 Homerton High Street, E9
Tel. 0208 986 2264
www.nationaltrust.org.uk
Open February to November, Wednesday and Sunday 11.30am to 5.30pm
Admission: £2.10
Nearest Tube: No Underground service nearby so take mainline train to Hackney Central

London's **oldest surviving house** was originally constructed in 1535 for one of Henry VIII's hitmen, Sir Ralph Sadleir, one of the judges at the trial of Mary, Queen of Scots - though it has been much altered since. There are Tudor, Stuart and Georgian interiors, with some particularly fine panelling.

Docklands
Nearest Tube: Canary Wharf

One of the most exciting and fastest growing urban developments in the world. The historic wharves, where ships once moored, have been superseded by spectacular high-tech offices, including the 850ft high **Canary Wharf** building, homes and shops. The wealth of leisure attractions, includes restaurants, pubs, wine bars, marinas, water sports centres, leafy tree-lined squares and cinemas.

Museum in Docklands
Warehouse No 1, West India Quay, E14
Tel. 0207 001 9800
www.museumindocklands.org.uk
Open daily 10am to 6pm. Admission: £5
Nearest Tube: Canary Wharf.
DLR: West India Quay

This newcomer to the long list of museums in London explores the story of **London's River, Port and People,** from Roman settlement of the port, through to the recent regeneration of London's former Docklands – a 2000 year storyline.

The Museum is located over five floors of a spectacular late Georgian warehouse on **West India Quay** – literally in the shadow of the Canary Wharf district - and offers twelve major galleries, a children's gallery, education services, functions suites, a restaurant and a shop. Galleries show how the region has been at the heart of centuries of social and economic change and pay homage to the people who helped to build and shape it – and those who continue to do so. Artifacts, engravings, paintings, testimonies and photos drawn from the outstanding collections of the Museum of London and the Port of London Authority, emphasise the skills and ingenuity of Dockland communities.

Hampstead, Highgate and Camden Town

Ultra-trendy **Camden Town**, with the highest concentration of twenty-somethings in London, is the sort of place where you'd come to get your navel or some other part of your anatomy pierced, or to purchase those clompy boots you'd always wanted. Antiques stores rub shoulders with fast-food hole-in-the-walls, and solicitors' offices sit uncomfortably next to tattoo emporia. At the northern end of the High Street, **Camden Lock** is in fact a pair of locks on **the Grand Union Canal**, that is also home to a huge market selling everything from clothing, crafts, and, inevitably, antiques.

One of London's prettiest neighborhoods, exclusive **Hampstead** was once a separate village, until plague-ridden Londoners started moving here to escape the filth of the city, some four miles away. So sought-after did the area become, that by the 18th century local spring water was being bottled and sold to city dwellers. The village became a firm favorite with writers and artists, and remains so to this day – with a significant smattering of media types. The steep **High Street**, with its designer shops, posh restaurants and trendy cafes, is attractive in itself, but for the prettiest bits, explore the streets to the east of the High Steet, like **Flask Walk**, and **Church Row**, with its elegant

Georgian town houses, and the 1745 church of St John, where the artist John Constable is buried. Then, of course, there's **Hampstead Heath**, a vast expanse of green – woods and fields, lakes and hills.

Hampstead Heath
Nearest Tube: Hampstead

Lying to the east of Hampstead Village, Hampstead Heath is one of the largest areas of urban open space in the world. What's so special about the Heath is the **diversity** of its landscape – utterly wild woodland, to rolling green hills and even a few lakes. There's are spectacular views toward the City and West End from 326ft **Parliament Hill** in the southern part of the Heath while Kenwood House contains a superb collection of 17th and 18th century art. (See Walks).

Freud Museum
20 Maresfield Gardens, NW3
Tel. 0207 435 2002
www.freud.org.uk
Open Wednesday to Sunday noon to 5pm
Admission £4
Nearest Tube: Finchley Road

This did, indeed, turn out to be his 'last address on this planet' as predicted by Freud

PUB TIPS

The Flask
77 Highgate West Hill, N6
Tel . 0208 340 7260
Nearest Tube: Highgate.

Pleasant place for lunch, but very crowded in the evenings.

The Spaniard's
Spaniard's Road, NW3
Tel. 0208 455 3276
Nearest Tube: Hampstead

It's a bit of a trek from the top of Hampstead High Street to the Spaniard's but worth the effort. Among its many visitors have been Charles Lamb, Dickens (of course), Keates, Shelley, Sir Joshua Reynolds and legendary highwayman Dick Turpin.

Freemason's Arms
32 Downshire Hill, NW3
Tel 0207 435 2127
Nearest Tube: Hampstead

Popular pub with reputedly the largest beer garden in Britain, complete with summerhouse, lawns and rose beds. ❖

himself. He only lived here a year before cancer struck (1939) but his spirit seems to linger on, especially in the study and consulting room with original carpets and fittings sent on from the house he fled in Vienna, including *that* **couch**. This is one of London's most evocative museums and as such is well worth a visit.

RESTAURANT TIPS

Café des Arts
82 Hampstead High Street, NW3
Tel. 0207 435 3608
Nearest Tube: Hampstead

Great place for no-frills good, mostly Mediterranean-style food at reasonable prices.

Camden Brasserie
216 Camden High Street, N1
Tel. 0207 482 2114
Nearest Tube: Camden Town

Real neighborhood family-run restaurant serving Mediterranean food, specializing in chargrilled meat. The decor is fairly simple, but attractive, and the staff friendly and helpful. ❋

Keats' House
Wentworth Place, Keats Grove, NW3
Tel. 0207 435 2062
www.keatshouse.org.uk
Open April to October Tuesday to Sunday, noon to 5pm; November to March, Tuesday to Sunday, noon to 4pm
Admission £3
Nearest Tube: Hampstead

Charming house near Hampstead Heath where the famous Romantic poet is celebrated with original manuscripts, letters – to the likes of William Wordsworth – and Keats' own collection of works by Shakespeare and Chaucer. Sadly the plum tree in the garden which inspired him to write *Ode to a Nightingale* is long gone.

Primrose Hill
At 206 feet, Primrose Hill, just north of Regent's Park, is one of the highest points in London, affording lovely views towards the City and West End. On **Bonfire Night** (otherwise known as Guy Fawkes' Night), November 5, the biggest bonfire in the city burns an effigy of the man who was accused of trying to blow up Parliament in 1606. Just round the corner, pretty **Regent's Park Road** is one of the most attractive village

streets in London, with a mixture of upmarket neighborhood shops, a collection of cafes just perfect for reading the book you've just purchased at **Primrose Hill Books**, one of the best-stocked small bookshops in London, and some decent restaurants.

Canal Museum
12-13 New Wharf Road, N1
Tel. 0207 713 0836
www.canalmuseum.org.uk
Open Tuesdays to Sundays 10am to 4.30pm
Admission: £3
Nearest Tube: Camden Town

A former ice warehouse built in 1862 for Carlo Gatti, a well-known ice cream maker, is the unlikely setting for this fascinating little museum which explores the history and development of London's **once-extensive canal network** which was one of the main reasons for the remarkable growth in trade and industry in the capital during the 18th and 19th centuries. Inside, you can see a narrowboat cabin, learn about the history of London's canals, the cargoes carried and the people who lived and worked on the waterways.

Jewish Museum
129-131 Albert Street, NW1
Tel. 0207 284 1997
www.jewmusm.ort.org
Open Monday to Thursday 10am to 4pm, Sunday 10am to 5pm
Admission: £3.50
Nearest Tube: Camden Town

Quirky museum which traces the history of the Jewish community in Britain from Norman times to the present day, and explores Jewish culture and traditions.

Highgate Cemetery
Swain's Lane, N6
Tel:0208 340 1834
www.highgate-cemetery.org
Open April to October Monday
to Friday 10am to 5pm, week-
ends 11am to 5pm; November
to March Monday to Friday
10am to4pm, weekends 11am
to 4pm
Admission: £2 (tour £3)
Nearest Tube: Highgate

This atmospheric, largely overgrown expanse, with its elaborate Gothic tombs, life-size angel statues and dark and gloomy crypts, is like something from a Hammer Horror flick. In reality, it's the last resting-place of a large number of luminaries, like **Karl Marx**, whose huge black bust is probably the most visited place. The novelist **George Eliot** and **Michael Faraday**, the scientist, are also buried here. While the main part of the cemetery – where most of the famous names are buried - is open to visitors, the more flamboyant western section is restricted. Tours by amazingly knowledgeable – and humorous – local guides are available at the main entrance.

Knightsbridge, Kensington and Chelsea

Knightsbridge, London's most expensive neighborhood, was the first place in the UK where the price of a house reached £50m. No wonder, when you look around the area, which is simply brimming with exclusive shops such as **Harrod's**, arguably the world's biggest department store, and **Sloane Street** with its English and French designer stores. South Kensington, just a short walk from here along Exhibition Road, is home to three of the world's finest museums, The **Victoria and Albert Museum** (V&A), a mecca for lovers of arts, crafts and design, the **Science Museum** and the **Natural History Museum**. Chelsea became famous in the 1960s as the focal point of 'swinging London.' The **King's Road** still brims with designer stores, cafes, pubs and restaurants, but you'll get a better feel for the place by exploring the side streets with their elegant Georgian townhouses and mews cottages.

Leighton House
12 Holland Park Road, W14
Tel. 0207 602 3316
www.rbkc.gov.uk/leightonhousemuseum
Open Monday to Saturday
11am to 5.30pm
Admission:£3
Nearest Tube: High Street Kensington

Frederic Leighton, Victorian painter, sculptor and sometime President of the Royal Academy, commissioned architect George Aitchison to build this house to show off his extensive **collection of art** in 1870. The focal point of the building is the amazing **Arab Hall**, based on 12th century reception hall of a Moorish palace. Exotic beyond belief, with marble columns, two-story jewelled dome and fountain, the hall is best known for its Islamic tiles, brought back by Leighton from North Africa, and by his explorer friend Richard Burton, whose translation of *Arabian Nights* raised many eyebrows in Victorian society. The rest of the house is not quite so extravagant; the **studio** and **library** are crammed

with fine paintings by Leighton himself and other leading pre-Raphaelites like Burne-Jones and Edward Millais.

Holland Park
Nearest Tube: High Street Kensington

The Jacobean **Holland House**, which was mostly destroyed by bombs during World War II, gives its name to this lovely park, a real oasis of trees, plants, flowers and lawns. The surviving east wing of the house is used as a youth hostel, and provides a stage for an **Open Air Theatre**, held from April to September. The **orangery** also survived and is now used for art exhibitions and for very upmarket wedding receptions, while the old Garden Ballroom is currently a restaurant. Other attractions include the formal **Dutch Garden**, designed in the 1790s, woodland areas, and pretty lawns where peacocks strut their stuff. A **rose garden** and a **Japanese Water Garden** complete the picture.

Notting Hill
Nearest Tube: Notting Hill

This area to the west of central London attained celebrity status almost overnight thanks to the 1999 blockbuster film of the same name, though the gentrification of the area pre-dates, rather than is the result of, the publicity the film generated. The area has not always been so trendy; in the 1960s it had a reputation as being a haven for drug pushers and violent gangs. Today Notting Hill is a relaxed, easy-going neighborhood of fine shops and boutiques, myriad modern art galleries, top-notch restaurants and happening bars and cafes – and with a distinct Afro-Caribbean atmosphere. The **Portobello Road**, with its antiques and bric-a-brac shops, is home to one of the world's best-known antiques markets, while every August Bank Holiday, the whole area comes alive with the biggest, most colorful street carnival in Europe, the **Notting Hill Carnival.**

Kensington Palace
Kensington Gardens, W8
Tel. 0207 937 9561
www.hrp.org.uk
Open March to October 10am to5pm, November to February 10am to 4pm
Admission: £8.80
Nearest Tube: Queensway

Once home to the late **Princess Margaret** and residence of **Diana, Princess of Wales** after her divorce from Prince Charles, this fine building, which dates from 1605, was bought by King William and Queen Mary in 1688. It was altered by architects Christopher Wren and Nicholas Hawksmoor and again when

FAST FOOD TIPS
Holland Park Café
Holland Park
Nearest Tube: High Street, Kensington

Run by an Italian family, this café is a great place to while a way an hour or two. Not surprisingly, Mediterranean dishes figure prominently, but you can get sandwiches and cakes. Their Café Latte is to die for.

Lisboa Patisserie
55 Golbourne Road, W10
Tel. 0208 968 5242
Nearest Tube: Ladbroke Grove

Just off the Portobello Road is this fantastic café which produces some of the best pastries – sweet and savory – in the capital. ❧

George I arrived from Hanover. Queen Victoria was born here in 1819 and it was here that, in June 1837 young Victoria was informed by the Archbishop of Canterbury and the Lord Chamberlain that her uncle, William IV had died, and that she was to be Queen.

Among the attractions inside the buildings are the **Royal Ceremonial Dress Collection**, including frocks worn by Diana herself. Check out the beautiful **Cupola Room**, where men were initiated into the noble Order of the Garter. Outside, the **Sunken Garden** is worth a peek, especially in the summer when it is a profusion of flowers; while the lovely **Orangery**, designed by Hawksmoor and Vanbrugh, and with carvings by Grinling Gibbons, now functions as a tea room.

Albert Memorial
Hyde Park, Kensington Gore, SW7
Tel. 0207 495 0916
Tours Sunday 2pm and 3pm.
Cost of tour: £3.50
Nearest Tube: South Kensington

This dazzling memorial to Queen Victoria's husband was erected by his grieving wife on the spot where **the Great Exhibition** – Albert's idea – had stood ten years before his 1861 death. The memorial, restored at great cost (£11m), was revealed to the public in 1998 after eight years under scaffolding, and the employment of what seems like several acres of gold leaf.

Princess Diana
Memorial Fountain
Near Alexandra Gate, Kensington Road, SW7
Nearest Tube: Knightsbridge or South Kensington

After many delays, the Diana, Princess of Wales Memorial Fountain flowed for the first time in July, 2004, after much criticism from Brits most of whom would have preferred something a little more substantial, and in a more central location than a quiet corner of Hyde Park. Costing £3.6 million ($9.43 million) to build, the fountain is shaped like a water-filled sloping stone ring, allowing visitors to splash in the water or picnic inside or around the oval.

American Kathryn Gustafson, whose design beat 57 other contenders said, "The princess was a contemporary woman and I wanted very much it to be a place you walked into. A total environment – not an object you walked around. She was so inclusive that we wanted it to be something you felt you were part of." Construction of the fountain, which is built out of 545 blocks of Cornish granite, was delayed by bureaucratic wrangling and arguments within the Memorial Fountain Committee. Soon after opening, the Fountain was closed again after a number of people slipped on the granite.

The Science Museum
Exhibition Road, SW7
Tel 020 7938 8080
www.sciencemuseum.org.uk
Open daily 10am to 6pm
Admission: £6.50
Nearest Tube: South Kensington

Geared primarily to schoolchildren, the Science Museum hardly inspires awe like its neighbor the Natural History Museum. But it's still a fascinating place, full of hands-on exhibits, and treasures including the **Puffing Billy**, the oldest train in the world, and the **Exploration of Space Exhibition**, with the original **Apollo 10** capsule on view. Better still is the **Land Transport** exhibit, loaded with trains, cars, including a **1909 Silver Ghost Rolls Royce**, buses, bicycles and motorcycles, a

RESTAURANT TIPS
Zafferano
15 Lowndes Street, SW1
Tel. 0207 235 5800
Nearest Tube:
Knightsbridge.

Zafferano is the greatest exponent of cucina nova in London. Try such ravishing delights as pumpkin ravioli, minced pork wrapped in Savoy cabbage leaves and monkfish with walnuts. For dessert, try Sardinian pecorino pastries served with unsweetened vanilla ice cream. Book early.

Bibendum
Michelin House, 81
Fulham Road, SW3
Tel. 0207 581 5817
Nearest Tube:
South Kensington

One of London's finest dining rooms, converted from an Edwardian garage. The menu is a mixture of traditional British, French and Italian dependables, and some more creative offerings, like smoked eel on a thin pancake. ❧

1910 horse-drawn coal trolley that still whiffs strongly of coal, and a huge 1923 Express locomotive. With sections on telecommunications, computing, nuclear physics and chemistry and a **History of Medicine Exhibit**, this is definitely the place for all would-be scientists – and anyone else who can't resist pressing buttons

Victoria and Albert Museum
Cromwell Road, SW7
Tel 0207 938 8441
www.vam.ac.uk
Open daily 10am to 5.45pm
Admission adults £5, seniors
£3, students and under 18s free
Nearest Tube: South Kensington

This museum prides itself on being the largest and most influential **decorative arts** museum in the world. Located on Cromwell Road in South Kensington, its **146**

galleries reflect centuries of achievement in such varied fields as ceramics, sculpture, furniture, jewelry and textiles.

This visually stunning Gothic building also contains the National Collections of sculpture, glass, ceramics, watercolors, portrait miniatures and photographs, and also houses the **National Art Library**.

Founded in 1852 as a Museum of Manufacturers its aim was to educate British manufacturers by building on the success of the previous year's **Great Exhibition**. It moved from Marlborough House where it became known as the Victoria and South Kensington Museum, later renamed the Victoria and Albert Museum in honor of the widowed Victoria's husband, whose brainchild it had been.

Among the museum's many treasures are the 12th century **Eltinberg Reliquary**, the early English **Gloucester candlestick**, ands the **Syon cope**, a priceless vestment woven in England in the 14th century.

The Natural History Museum
Cromwell Road, SW7
Tel 0207 942 5000
www. Nhm.ac.uk

Open Monday to Saturday 10am to 5.50pm, Sunday 11am to 5.50pm
Admission adults £6, children £3, under 5s free
Nearest Tube: South Kensington.

This massive Victorian cathedral of natural history - the most visited of all the London museums - is located next door to the V&A in Cromwell Road. Enter, and you'll be met by a huge 80ft long, 150 million year old **diplodocus** dinosaur, surrounded by glass cases containing **fossils** of various creatures – such as lions, elephants and bears – associated with Africa and Asia today but which millions of years ago roamed free in the area you're now standing.

Kids (but maybe not mom) will love the **Creepy Crawlies Gallery**, with its gigantic enlarged scorpion and a host of cuddly taratulas, and everyone will be thrilled by the **Earth Galleries**, where, among other things, you can see a mock-up of a shop damaged during the 1995 earthquake at Kobe, Japan. As with its neighbor, the V&A, your biggest problem will be where to start.

SHOPPING TIP
Harrods
87-135 Brompton Road, SW1
Tel. 0207 730 1234
www.harrods.co.uk
Open Monday to Saturday 10am to 7pm.
Closed Sunday
Nearest Tube: Knightsbridge.

The world's most famous department store, established in 1849, is a massive, 15-acre six-story Edwardian terracotta pile, illuminated at night by thousands of white lights. The store's motto is *Omnia, omnibus, ubique* (Latin for "everything, for everyone, everywhere"). Most visitors make a bee-line for the legendary Food Hall, with its stunning art nouveau tiling, and unbelievable displays of fish, meat and vegetables and breads. Whether you intend to make a serious purchase here, or have simply come to rub shoulders with the rich and famous, you must make sure to come away with at least one item – a green and gold Harrods carrier bag.

Brompton Oratory
Brompton Road, SW7
Tel. 0207 808 0900
www.brompton-oratory.org.uk.
Open daily 9am to 5pm
Admission: free
Nearest Tube: South Kensington.

Usually known simply as 'The Oratory,' this ranks as the second largest Roman Catholic Church in London after Westminster Cathedral. It was established in 1884 by Cardinal Newman, whose statue stands outside. An almost-unknown young architect, Herbert Gribble, won a competition to design the building. He certainly went to town! The awesome interior is incredibly ornate, and several treasures far older than the building itself bear witness to the growing wealth of the Roman Church in England at this time. Check out the giant **Twelve Apostles** in the nave, carved out of Carrara marble in the 1680s and transposed here from Siena cathedral.

Chelsea & Greenwich

For some background history, see Walks: Chelsea.

National Army Museum
Royal Hospital Road, SW3
Tel. 0207 730 0717
www.national-army-museum.ac.uk
Open daily 10am to 5.30pm
Admission: free
Nearest Tube: Sloane Square

Not to be confused with the far more impressive Imperial War Museum (see South Bank section) the National Army Museum focuses on the history of the British land forces from the establishment of the Yeomen of the Guard (forerunners of the 'Beefeaters) in 1485, to current military operations. Among the displays are dozens of military uniforms and medals, a scale model of the **Battle of Waterloo**, where 48,000 lost their lives, and the skeleton of Marengo, Napoleon's charger at Waterloo. Hitler's phone switchboard and a collection of paintings by Turner and Gainsborough are also here.

The Royal Hospital
Royal Hospital Road, SW3
Tel. 0207730 0161
www.chelsea-pensioners.org.uk
Open Monday to Saturday
10am to noon and 2pm to 4pm,
Sunday 2pm to 4pm
Admission: free
Nearest Tube: Sloane Square

King Charles II commissioned eminent architect Sir Christopher Wren to design this hospice for elderly and infirm veterans in 1682 – some say because he'd been badgered into doing so by his mistress Nell Gwynne, others because of restlessness among the armed forces after several exhausting military campaigns, poor pensions and care. The result was this magnificent red-brick and Portland stone building, which became the model for similar institutional architecture the world over.

The central courtyard contains a bronze statue by Grinling Gibbons of Charles II in Roman garb. On Oak Apple Day (May 29) the 'Chelsea pensioners' – war veterans who reside in the Hospital – cover the statue with oak leaves to remember the occasion in 1651 when Charles I hid in an oak tree to escape the parliamentary forces of Cromwell. The giant Tuscan portico off the courtyard leads to Wren's beautiful but austere Chapel, while opposite is the dining hall, all wooden paneled, where the Pensioners still have their meals. A small museum in the Secretary's Office has displays of Pensioners' costumes and medals.

> **RESTAURANT TIP**
> **Chelsea Kitchen**
> *98 King's Road, SW3*
> *Tel. 0207 589 1330*
> *Nearest Tube:*
> *Sloane Square*
>
> No frills restaurant where you can get a two or three course meal for well under £10. As you'd expect, it's very basic – pasta, omelettes, stews and suchlike. ❧

Chelsea Physic Garden
66 Royal Hospital Road, SW3
Tel. 0207 352 5646
www.cpgarden.demon.co.uk

Open April to October Wednesday noon to 5pm, Sunday 2pm to 6pm
Admission: £4
Nearest Tube: Sloane Square.

In 1673, members of the **Apothecaries Society** livery company created the garden to study the connection between botany and medicine. It's a hauntingly beautiful place, a real Secret Garden with acres of sunken beds containing more than 7,000 species of plants, many of them rare. Perfume plants, medicinal plants and poison plants abound. Britain's largest (and therefore probably oldest) olive tree is also resident. Note the (very) limited opening hours.

Carlyle's House
24 Cheyne Row, SW3
Tel. 0207 352 7087
www.nationaltrust.org.uk
Open April to early November, Wednesdays and Sundays only, 11am to 5pm
Admission £3.50
Nearest Tube: Sloane Square

Lovely Queen Anne style house where the essayist – famed for his history of the French Revolution - lived. You can see the spartan kitchens down below and the study where he put pen to paper,

RESTAURANT TIPS
La Tante Claire
68 Royal Hospital Rd
Tel. 0207 352 6045
Nearest Tube:
Sloane Square
Jacket and tie required

Famous, top-notch restaurant, with superb food, an excellent wine list and impeccable service.

Blue Elephant
4-6 Fulham Broadway
Tel. 0207 385 6595
Nearest Tube:
Fulham Broadway

This Thai restaurant is a bit of a stretch from Chelsea, but worth the effort. It's like a set from the film *The King and I*. There are real fishponds (with live carp – any on the menu?), lots of thatch, bamboo, waterfalls and palm trees, along with sarong-clad waitresses. And the food? Well, it's good. If you're famished after a traipse around the museums, opt for the 17-dish Royal Thai banquet. ❖

and the drawing room where he and other eminent writers

of his day – Dickens, Thackeray, Tennyson and Browning - used to meet for a chinwag.

PUB TIP
The King's Head and Eight Bells
50 Cheyne Walk, SW3
Tel. 0207 352 1820
Nearest Tube:
Sloane Square

Historic riverside pub that oozes with character, and is just a stone's throw from the residences of some of London's best-known former citizens – Thomas Carlyle and George Eliot, to name just a couple. There's a wide range of English beers on sale, and the quality of the food is several notches higher than your average hostelry. *

Greenwich
Greenwich, the place from which the world's time is measured, is a quaint, village-like destination in its own right that, as Maritime Greenwich received the accolade of **World Heritage Site** in 1997. Most visitors to Greenwich, however, head straight for the **National Maritime Museum**,

a vast collection of seafaring artifacts, ranging from ship's maps and charts to ships themselves. The Museum's aim is to tell the story of Britain's obsession with the sea, and it does so with some success.

National Maritime Museum, Greenwich
Romney Road, SE10
Tel. 0208 312 6565
www.nmm.ac.uk
Open 10am to 5pm
Admission: free
Nearest Tube: London Docklands Railway Cutty Sark Station

To mark the millennium, the Museum's central courtyard was covered with a massive, single-span glass roof to link more than 20 themed galleries on two of the museum's three levels. The galleries have plenty of interactive displays and video art that deals with subjects ranging from the rum trade and slavery, to marine ecology and the future of the oceans. Check out the **Nelson Gallery**, on the third floor, which tells the story of Nelson's great battles – Trafalgar and The Nile. You can see the tunic the great man was wearing when he was shot – with bullet hole in the fabric – as well as the actual bullet.

Children are kept occupied with an on-board interactive display on ship's gunnery, signalling and deep sea diving. Adjacent to the Museum is the magnificent **Queen's House**, a Palladian mansion that was once home to King Charles I, with exhibits featuring illustrious seafarers.

Royal Observatory
Greenwich Park, SE10
Tel. 0208 312 6565
www.nmm.ac.uk
Open 10am to 5pm
Admission: free
Nearest Tube: London Docklands Railway Cutty Sark Station

Not far from the National Maritime Museum is the place where the world's time has been measured since 1884: Here it is that the planet divides between east and west and you can put your feet either side the line and straddle both hemispheres! The Observatory itself is a rather lovely Wren construction, built in 1675 for John Flamsteed, Charles II's astronomer, and used by successive royal astronomers until 1948. Inside is an interesting display of telescopes, quadrants and other astronomical gear, along with the world's seventh largest refracting telescope, built in 1893.

RESTAURANT TIPS
The North Pole
131 Greenwich High Road, SE10
Tel. 0207 853 3020
Nearest Tube: Greenwich

The food has been described as 'East meets West' which roughly translated means Pacific Rim style with European ingredients, so – pan-fried monkfish comes on a coconut and coriander rice cake. Get my drift?

The Spread Eagle
2 Stockwell Street, SE10
Tel. 0208 853 2333
Nearest Tube: Greenwich

The Spread Eagle dates back to the 17th century, with a slanting floor that makes you feel you're on board a ship – appropriately, it seems – this is Greenwich. The menu is an appealing mixture of French and English cuisine, the ambiance friendly and relaxed. ❧

Cutty Sark

Cutty Sark Gardens, King William Walk, SE10
Tel. 0208 858 3445
www.cuttysark.org.uk
Open daily 10am to 5pm
Admission: £3.50. (Cutty Sark)
£1 (Gipsy Moth)
DLR: Cutty Sark

The *Cutty Sark* was easily the fastest ship in the world the seven seas when launched in 1869, sailing the London to China route on one occasion in only 107 days The former tea clipper is now permanently moored in a dry dock alongside the Thames. You can explore its teak-lined cabins, stroll the decks and admire the amusing collection of figureheads. Close by, the *Gipsy Moth IV* is the boat in which Sir Francis Chichester was the first sailor to single-handedly circumnavigate the world in 1966. See the cramped cabin where he spent 226 days and the clever way everything was stored.

Wehrner Collection at Ranger's House

Chesterfield Walk, Blackheath, SE10
Tel. 0208 853 0035
www.english-heritage.org.uk
Open June to August Wednesday to Sunday 10am to 5pm; September to May: pre-booked tours only

Admission: £4.50
Nearest Tube: Cutty Sark or mainline train from Victoria to Greenwich

Diamond magnate Sir Julius Wehrner, who died in 1912, spent millions on putting together this fabulous collection of more than 700 works of art. The collection is based around twelve elegant 18th century rooms in a former park ranger's house and includes minutely carved and painted medieval gothic ivories, a fine collection of porcelain and high quality Renaissance decorative arts, inclduing more than 100 Renaissance jewels, making it one of the finest collections of **jewelry** in Europe.

Fan Museum

12 Crooms Hill, SE10
Tel. 0208 305 1441
www.fan-museum.org
Open Tuesday to Sunday 11am to 5pm, Sunday noon to5pm
Admission: £3.50
DLR: Cutty Sark. Train: Greenwich Station (from Charing Cross or Waterloo East)

This highly unusual museum possesses the world's most important single collection of more than 2,000 fans, some dating from the17th century, with displays illustrating their history, development – and purpose. The collection, along with a workshop and conservation center, was set up in 1991 and is housed in a pair of exquisite 1721 buildings, recently restored to retain their original character and elegance.

An Orangery, faithful to the architecture of the period, overlooks a "secret" garden in the Japanese style, with a fan shaped parterre, pond, stream and oriental architectural features – a real oasis of tranquility.

The South Bank

Lambeth Palace
Lambeth Palace Road, SE1
www.archbishopofcanterbury.org/
palace
Museum of Garden History open March to mid-December, Monday to Friday 11am to 3pm, weekends 10.30am to 5pm
Admission: free, but suggested donation: £3.50
Nearest Tube: Westminster.
www.cix.co.uk/~museumgh.

Since the 13th century Lambeth Palace has been the London residence of the **Archbishop of Canterbury**, spiritual head of the Anglican Communion. Located on the south bank, almost opposite St Thomas Hospital, the Palace is rarely open to the public, but you can admire the fine **Tudor gateway** from the outside. Adjacent to the Palace, **St Mary's Church**, deconsecrated in

1977, is owned by the **Tradescant Trust**, named for botanist John Tradescant, who introduced to Britain a variety of now commonplace plants that he discovered on his travels round the world – plants like the lilac, jasmine and larch. The **Museum of Garden History** was set up here in his honor, and contain a range of horticultural exhibits, including a replica of a 17th century knot garden. Near Tradescant's tomb, in the graveyard, is the final resting place of William Bligh, of Bounty fame.

Florence Nightingale Museum
Lambeth Palace Road, SE1
Tel. 0207 620 0374
www.florence-nightingale.co.uk
Open Monday to Friday 10 to 5pm, Saturday 10am to 4.30pm
Admission: £5
Nearest Tube: Westminster

This museum, dedicated to **'The Lady with the Lamp'** started life as part of the School of Nursing at St. Thomas's Hospital, one of London's great teaching hospitals, which Florence Nightingale herself founded in 1860. The museum contains her personal effects, including items of clothing, books and letters, as well as mementoes from the Crimean War in which she made her name. There's a reconstruction of a **ward in a field hospital** in Scutari (Turkey) and an **East End slum** cottage showing how she helped improve the lot of the poor in London's East End.

Imperial War Museum
Lambeth Road, SE1
Tel. 0207 416 5320
www.iwm.org.uk
Open daily 10am to 6pm
Admission free (but special exhibitions may require fee)
Nearest Tube: Lambeth North

This old museum occupies the former asylum known as 'Bedlam' offers a well-put-together, child-friendly experience that avoids glamorizing its subject. Of course, there's all the stuff you'd expect to find in a war museum; **Spitfires,** a Polaris missile, even part of the Messerschmidt flown by **Rudolph Hess.** You can even look through the eyepiece of a German mast periscope, first used in 1917, offering a bird's eye view of London.

It's the **lower level** that's the more stimulating, with dozens of interactive exhibits, German propaganda films on the invasion of Europe, a moving account of life in London during the Blitz taken with a home movie camera, and an even more moving film of the liberation of **Belsen Camp.** The highlight of the museum is the **Blitz Experience** – a recreation of life in London during an enemy air raid that starts in a cramped bunker with all the associated sound effects. When the siren gives the all-clear, you can wander out and witness the devastation. **The Trench Experience**, depicting life in a World War I trench and **Operation Jericho**, a simulated RAF flight across occupied Europe, are also worth seeing. The museum's biggest draw these days is the **Holocaust Exhibition**, which opened in 2003, on the third floor. Upstairs are galleries, a self-service **cafe** and a gift shop.

London Aquarium
County Hall, Westminster Bridge Road, SE1

Tel. 0207 967 8000
www.londonaquarium.co.uk
Open daily 10am to 6pm
Admission: £6.50
Nearest Tube: Waterloo

The London Aquarium is housed in the old **County Hall** building, on the opposite bank of the Thames from the Houses of Parliament. Though it cannot compare with, say New England Aquarium in Boston, or Sydney Aquarium (mainly because it's not in a purpose built building) it is, however, a great place to take the kids on a wet afternoon when the view from the Millennium Wheel next door is non-existent. Visitors are submerged in a stunning display of hundreds of varieties of fish and sea life from around the world, including piranhas and sharks, and there's a particularly well-designed jellyfish tank containing hundreds of the slimy submersibles from the world's oceans all lit up with ultra violet light.

Saatchi Gallery
County Hall, Westminster Bridge Road, SE1
Tel. 0207 928 8195
www.saatchi-gallergy.co.uk
Open Sunday to Thursday 10am to 8pm, Friday and Saturday 10am to 10pm

Admission: £8.75
Nearest Tube: Waterloo

The new Saatchi Gallery is one of London's leading venues for **contemporary art**. Charles Saatchi, he of the famous advertising company, and one of the world's leading collectors, is constantly searching for new talent and his sometimes controversial choices never fail to intrigue and even shock. The Gallery's main focus is on contemporary British artists like Tracey Emin and Damien Hirst.

Dali Universe
County Hall, Westminster Bridge Road, SE1
Tel. 0207 620 2720
www.daliuniverse.com
Open daily 10am to 6.30pm
Admission: £9
Nearest Tube: Waterloo

The dissolution of the Greater London Council by Mrs Thatcher's government in the late 1980s has resulted in this huge building, facing the Houses of Parliament, being given over to a variety of uses, from hotels, to cafes, restaurants and even an aquarium. One of the attractions it now houses is this gallery given over primarily to the works of Salvador Dali. Among the 500 works of art on display is the famous Mae West Lips. The gallery also hosts original works by Picasso and Chagall.

The London Eye (Millennium Wheel)
Jubilee Gardens, SE1
Tel. 0870 500 0600
www.ba-londoneye.com
Open January to April and October 9.30am to 8pm; May to September 9.30am to 10pm
Admission: £8.50
Nearest Tube: Westminster

This huge ferris wheel – the largest of its kind in the world – was finally hauled upright a few weeks after schedule New Year's Eve, 1999/2000. Since opening, the 450ft high wheel, with its 32 glass capsules, has become one of London's most popular tourist attractions. The wheel moves round extremely slowly (one revolution takes around 20 minutes) affording passengers spectacular views over the whole city and beyond. It's a great place to start your London visit.

The South Bank Centre
The South Bank, SE1
Tel 020 7960 4242
www.sbc.org.uk
Nearest Tube: Embankment, (then walk across the Hungerford pedestrian bridge to the South Bank) or Waterloo (follow well-marked signs out of the station to 'South Bank')

This sprawling concrete and glass complex covers several acres next to the Thames. It houses three important concert halls – the **Royal Festival Hall**, **Queen Elizabeth Hall** and **Purcell Room** – and three theaters – the **Lyttleton**, **Cottesloe** and **Olivier**, as well as the **National Film Theatre**, and the **Hayward Gallery**, where top-notch traveling exhibitions are held. There are several places to eat here, including a couple of café-bars that overlook the Thames.

Museum of the Moving Image
Below Waterloo Bridge
Tel. 0207 401 2636
www. Bfi.org.uk/momi
Open daily 10am to 6pm
Admission: £5
Nearest Tube: Waterloo

Located under Waterloo Bridge, **MOMI** as it's known is a quirky, fun museum with lots of hands-on displays that will keep children happy for hours. Of course there's the obligatory history of film and cinema, with real life actors on hand to add a touch of awe, and dozens of memorabilia such as cameras, posters and costumes, but the real fun starts further on, where you can audition for a screen test, make your own cartoons in the animation room, and visit a Hollywood film set, complete with autocratic director. There's loads of newsreel and archive covering major international events like the Hindenberg disaster and a TV section where budding Dan Rathers can strut their stuff.

RESTAURANT TIP

Oxo Tower Restaurant
Oxo Tower Wharf,
Barge House Street,
SE1
Tel. 0207 803 3888
Nearest Tube:
Blackfriars (you'll need
to walk across
Blackfriars Bridge)

The Oxo Tower Restaurant, Bar & Brasserie is situated on the eighth floor of the Oxo Tower. The central tower divides the space into two equal halves, to the east, The Oxo Tower Restaurant and to the west, The Oxo Tower Bar and Brasserie. Both are linked by a spectacular 250-foot terrace offering spectacular views across The River towards The City.

❧

Bankside Gallery
48 Hopton Street, SE1
Tel. 0207 928 7521
www.banksidegallery.com
Open Tuesday 10am to 8pm;
Wednesday to Friday 10am to
5pm; weekends 11am to 5pm
Admission: £3.50
Nearest Tube: Waterloo

The home of the Royal Watercolour Society and the **Royal Society of Painter-Printmakers** has no permanent collection, but houses constantly-changing exhibitions of watercolors, engravings and prints.

Tate Modern
Located at Bankside, SE1
Tel 020 7887 8000
Open Sunday to Thursday
10am to 6pm, Friday and Saturday 10am to 10pm
Admission free, but donation welcome
Nearest Tune: Blackfriars or Southwark.

Even if you can't stand modern art, this **breathtaking new gallery** is well worth a visit. The Tate Modern displays part of what is a much larger collection of art that is shared with Tate Galleries in Liverpool, St Ives (Cornwall) and just along the Thames. This collection of modern art from 1900 to the present in a converted power station that had been an eyesore for years. The emptied-out former **Turbine Hall** runs the length of the building is now its awe-inspiring setting for temporary exhibits. From here, you're swept up by escalator through two floors, featuring a café, shops and auditorium to three levels of galleries. Galleries are located on the third, fourth and fifth floors of the building. Thematically-arranged exhibitions from the gallery's permanent collection are located on the third and fifth floors, while temporary exhibitions are located on the fourth floor.

At the top of the building is a two-story glass roof providing natural light for the galleries and for an excellent **café** with stunning views over London. And the art? Well, among the amazing collection of pieces on display are works by Bacon, Dali, Matisee, Picasso and Warhol, to name but a few. This truly is one of London's greatest attractions and is a must-see for anyone who is even remotely interested in art.

The Globe Theatre
21 New Globe Walk, SE1
Tel. 0207 902 1500 (Theater performance information: 020 7401 9919)

www.shakespeares-globe.org
Open May to September daily 9am to noon; October to April 10am to 5pm
Admission adults £6.50, seniors and students £5, children £4.50
Nearest Tube: London Bridge

Shakespeare's original Globe was about 200 yards away from its replacement, which was opened in 1996 in New Globe Walk, thanks to the unstinting efforts of American actor Sam Wanamaker, who was shocked to find that there was no permanent memorial to the Bard in London. Authentic Elizabethan methods were used to build the theater, and the first thatched roof in London since the Great Fire was a popular finishing touch. Plays are presented in natural light to up to 1,000 people on wooden benches and a further 500 groundlings standing on a carpet of shells, as they did 400 years ago. The theater is open for performance only in the summer, but guided tours are available year round from the **Globe Exhibition Centre** next door.

Vinopolis
1 Bank End, SE1
Tel. 0870 241 4040
www.vinopolis.co.uk
Open Monday, Friday and Saturday, noon to 9pm; Tuesday

to Thursday and Sunday noon to 6pm
Admission: £12.50
Nearest Tube: London Bridge

Suitable both for wine connoisseurs and those who simply enjoy a glass of the stuff, Vinopolis, housed in an old wine warehouse sets out to 'take away the mysteries of wine.'

Armed with an audio-guide and tasting tokens, visitors spend at least two hours within the Vinopolis experience. Discover Chianti on a Piaggio Vespa and the Australian wine regions on board the Vinopolis aeroplane. Drink your way through the world of wine and lead your senses on an exploration of hidden aromas and tastes. All this, in London?

The Golden Hinde
St. Mary Overie Dock, Cathedral Street, SE1
Open daily, but call 08700 118700 for exact times
www.goldenhinde.co.uk
Admission: self-guided tour: £2.75, guided tour (prebook required): £3.50
Nearest Tube: London Bridge

Sir Francis Drake, one of Britain's most famous mariners, circumnavigated the world in the original *Golden Hinde* from 1577 to 1580. This reconstruction boasts five galleries, including a gun deck and 22 cannons. Crew members are in period dress and there's an exhibition describing the life of seafarer in the 16th century, along with a number of nautical artifacts from the period. The ship is open daily for guided or self-guided tours.

Museum of Tea and Coffee
1 Maguire Street, SE1
Tel. 0207 403 5650

www.bramahmuseum.co.uk
Open daily 10am to 6pm
Admission: £4
Nearest Tube: Tower Hill

This quirky, unusual little museum traces the history of tea and coffee drinking in the UK and is the world's first museum devoted entirely to the **history of tea and coffee**. It tells the commercial and social 400 year old history of two of the world's most important beverages since their arrival in Europe from the Far East and Africa. The London tea trade conducted the business of unloading ships, marketing, blending and packing on both sides of the Thames close to London Bridge. Although the tea auctions were held north of the river, the South Bank boasted many prestigious warehouses, including nearby Butler's Wharf where once more than 6,000 chests of tea were handled every day.

Southwark Cathedral
Borough High Street
Tel 020 7367 6700
www.dswark.org
Open daily from 8.30am to 4pm
Admission donation
Nearest Tube: London Bridge

South London's main Anglican cathedral, Southwark is

> **SHOPPING TIP**
> **Borough Market**
> *8 Southwark Street, SE1*
> *Tel. 0207 407 1002*
> *Open Friday noon to 6pm, Saturday 9am to 4pm*
> *Nearest Tube: London Bridge*
>
> Specialist farmers travel from all over the country to sell their wares here and the market has quite a reputation amongst London's 'foodies', as well as top chefs and restaurateurs. Where else in central London can you buy in one place: pork, ham, wild boar, venison, ostrich, game, poultry, beef, fish, olives, cheeses, wines and beers (many organic), speciality bread, fruit and vegetables? ❋

the second-oldest Gothic church in London after Westminster Abbey, with some parts dating back to the 12th century. It only became a cathedral in 1905, having previously been known as the Priory Church of St Mary Overie (which means 'over the water') Inside, there's a fine **nave** and **medieval screen**. Look out for the rather gaudy 1408 tomb of poet John Gower, a friend of Geoffrey Chaucer, and the chapel dedicated to **John Harvard**, founder of Harvard University, who was baptized here in 1608.

Another slab marks the last resting-place **of Edmund Shakespeare**, brother of William, while a more evocative recent memorial commemorates the victims of the 1988 *Marchioness* disaster, when a pleasure craft hit a bridge nearby and sank in the Thames, drowning some 30 partygoers. The cathedral is the venue for some excellent lunchtime recitals by well-known organists and choirs.

London Dungeon
28-34 Tooley Street, SE1
Tel. 0208 403 7221
www.pool-of-london.co.uk
Open daily April to September 10am to 6.30pm; October to March 10am to 5.30pm
Admission: £10.95
Nearest Tube: London Bridge

Some of the grisliest events in Britain's history are recalled at this gloomy cavern under the railway arches, where you can see reconstructions of hangings at Tyburn, Anne Boleyn's beheading. Jack the Ripper naturally features quite prominently in the proceedings, and the most recent addition takes you on a boat ride through Traitor's gate at the Tower to the dungeon. What fun!

Old Operating Theatre
9a St Thomas Street, SE1
Tel. 0207 955 4791

PUB TIP
George Inn
77 Borough High Street, SE1
Tel. 0207 407 2056
Nearest Tube: Borough

Just a few yards from Southwark Cathedral, this beautiful galleried building was constructed in the late 17th century, and overlooks a courtyard where Shakespeare plays were once performed. In fact, legend says that the Bard actually drank here – it's certainly not far from the Globe Theatre. Dickens was another regular. Inside, it's an intricate maze of rooms, passageways, hidden bars and a restaurant. ❧

www.thegarret.org.uk
Open daily 10am to 5pm
Admission £3.50
Nearest Tube: London Bridge

Located in a garret atop the tower of St Thomas's Church, this unusual museum illustrates, by means of some rather gory reconstructions, how operations and other medical treatments were conducted (or perhaps meted out would be a better way of putting it) in the 19th century. The garret was once used by St Thomas's Hospital (now located opposite the Houses of Parliament) as an apothecary.

HMS Belfast
Morgan's Lane, Tooley Street, SE1
Tel. 0207 940 6300
www.iwm.org.uk/belfast
Open March to October daily 10am to 6pm, November to February daily 10am to 5pm
Admission: £5
Nearest Tube: London Bridge

World War II battleship that was decommissioned in the 1960s and is now moored on the Thames just a few minutes from Southwark Cathedral. *HMS Belfast* is a cruiser. She was launched in March 1938 and served throughout the Second World War, playing a leading part in the destruction of the German battle cruiser *Scharnhorst* at the Battle of North Cape and in the Normandy Landings.

After the war, she supported United Nations forces in Korea and remained in service with the Royal Navy until 1965. In 1971 she was saved for the nation as a unique and historic reminder of Britain's naval heritage in the first half of the twentieth century.

A tour round this huge and complex warship takes you from her quarterdeck up to the top of the bridge and all the way down through nine decks to her massive boiler and engine rooms. On the

RESTAURANT TIP
Butler's Wharf Chop House
36e Shad Thames
Tel. 0207 403 3403
Nearest Tube: Tower Hill or London Bridge

The Chop House prides itself on using only the best British produce. What's great about this place is that no-one bats an eyelid if it's an extravagant binge you're after, or a simple dish at the bar.

way you will see her triple six-inch gun turrets, the heavily armoured shell rooms and magazines and experience what life was like for her crew by visiting the cramped mess decks, officers' cabins, galley and sick bay.

City Hall

The Queen's Walk, SE1
www. London-gov.uk
Open Monday to Friday 8am to 8pm
Admission: free
Nearest Tube: London Bridge

This controversial new building was constructed in 2002 as the headquarters of the Greater London Authority and the main office of the elected Mayor of London (not to be confused with the Lord Mayor of London, whose jurisdiction consists solely of the square mile City). The striking ten-story glass building includes the London **Photomat**, an aerial view across London, on the ground floor, as well as a library and visitor center, while on the top floor, a viewing platform gives superb views of the city.

Design Museum

28 Shad Thames, SE1
Tel. 0207 940 8790
www.designmuseum.org
Open daily 10am to 5.45pm
Admission £6
Nearest Tube: Tower Hill

Converted from a former warehouse, the sparkling white Design Museum was founded to showcase industrial and domestic design and contains an assortment of exhibits ranging from telephones to cars of the present and future, vacuum cleaners and household furniture (including a wicker chair you can pick up with one finger).

FAST FOOD TIP
The Blue Print Café
28 Shad Thames, SE1.
Tel. 0207 378 7031
Nearest Tube: Tower Hill

Part of the Design Museum, the Blue Print Café has a great terrace overlooking The River.
�֍

Off the Beaten Path

Eltham Palace
Court Road, SE9
Tel. 0208 294 2548
www.english-heritage.co.uk
Open April to September
Wednesday to Friday and Sunday 10am to 6pm; October same days, 10am to 5pm; November to March, same days 10am to 4pm
Admission: £6
Nearest Tube: no nearby Tube station, but take mainline train to Eltham Station

This very unusual Tudor palace was the boyhood home of Henry VIII. Its **Great Hall** was originally built for Edward IV in the 1470s, but the moat is even older. It's unusual, because for many years it lay as a virtual ruin, until a member of the Courtauld family turned it into a luxury home in the 1930s. All the latest innovations were incorporated, including an audio system, centralised vacuum cleaner and under-floor heating.

The **dining room** is stunning, with pink leather-upholstered chairs, bird's-eye maple-veneered walls and a silver ceiling. More exotic still is the vaulted **bathroom**, lined with onyx and gold mosaic, with gold-plated bath taps and a statue of the goddess Psyche. Nineteen acres of beautiful **gardens** surround the palace.

Wimbledon Lawn Tennis Museum
Gate 4, Church Road, SW19
Tel. 0208 946 6131
www.wimbledon.org
Open daily 10.30am to 5pm
Admission: £5
Nearest Tube: Southfields

It's a bit of a trek from central London, but well worth a visit if tennis is your game. On display here are all kinds of tennis artifacts and memorabilia, from the invention of the mower (crucially, Wimbledon is played on grass!) to the development of the tennis ball. In the 1850s. Famous moments from the tournaments history are relived in a sight-and-sound presentation.

Dulwich Picture Gallery
Gallery Road, London SE21
Tel. 0208 693 5254
www.dulwichpicturegallery.org.uk
Open Tuesday to Friday 10am

to 5pm, weekends 11am to 5pm
Admission £4
Nearest Tube: No Tube service here, so take main line from Victoria to Dulwich Station

Designed by eminent architect Sir John Soane between 1811-1815, this is one of the oldest and finest purpose-built galleries ever built. Housed inside are masterpieces by the likes of Canaletto, Rembrandt, Rubens, Reynolds and Gainsborough. It's a bit of a trek from downtown London, but well worth the effort.

Chiswick House
Burlington Lane, W4
Tel. 0208 995 0508
www.engligh-heritage.org.uk/london
Open April 1 to October 31 Wednesday to Sunday 10am to 5pm (but closes 2pm on Saturdays)
Nearest Tube: Richmon
Train: St Margaret's

One of Britain's finest examples of 18th century domestic architecture, Chiswick House was built by the third Earl of Burlington, a well-traveled man who attempted to recreate the type of house and garden found in ancient Rome. With its beautiful **classical façade**, the house contains an octagonal central hall with impressive dome. The **Blue Velvet Room** has some superb gilding. The stunning Italianate gardens are speckled with classical temples and statues. There's a pretty lake and a conservatory with a collection of rare 19th century camellias.

Hogarth's House
Hogarth Lane
Tel. 0208 994 6757
Open Tuesday to Friday 1pm to 5pm, Saturday and Sunday 1pm to 6pm
Admission: Free
Nearest Tube: Richmond
Train: St Margaret's

Uncomfortably close to a busy six-lane highway, this house – once an idyllic rural retreat – is where the painter, engraver and satirist William Hogarth lived for 15 years until he died in 1764. Displays retell the story of Hogarth's life and explain his strong beliefs – including his abhorrence of cruelty to animals and children and his opinions on alcohol, symbolised in his famous painting *Gin Lane*. The house contains examples of his best work, like the wickedly satirical stories told *in The Rake's Progress* and *The Harlot's Progress*. The beautiful garden, with its ancient mulberry tree, is a sea of calm in a busy neighborhood.

Horniman Museum
100 London Road, SE23
Tel. 0208 699 1872
www.horniman.ac.uk
Open Monday to Saturday,
10.30am to 5.30pm, Sunday
2pm-5.30pm
Admission: free
Tube: No Tube service available locally, so take main line train to Forest Hill station

This unusual, but captivating small museum is some way from central London, but well worth the effort, especially if you're interested in African and Afro-Caribbean culture and art. Among the displays are **African Worlds**, the UK's first permanent gallery of the latter, a **Music Room** displaying myriad musical instruments and what they sound like, and an **aquarium**.

RAF Museum, Hendon
Grahame Park Way, NW9
Tel. 0208 8205 2266
www.rafmuseum.org
Open daily 10am to 6pm
Admission: free
Nearest Tube: Colindale

Situated on the site of the historic London Aerodrome, the RAF Museum consists of a collection of more than **90 aircraft**, aviation artifacts and memorabilia, including classic planes like the Lancaster, Wellington and Valiant, Visitors can experience the sights and sounds of **The Blitz**, The 'Friendly Invasion' exhibit tells the story of the **US Air Force in Britain** during World War II.

Thames Flood Barrier
1 Unity Way, SE18
Tel. 0208 305 4188
www.environment-agency.co.uk
Open Monday to Friday 10am to 5pm, weekends 10.30am to 5.30pm
Admission: £3.40
Nearest Tube: No Tube service nearby, co take mainline service to Charlton. There are also boat services to the barrier from piers in central London

London has always been prone to flooding, and the combination of high tide and a strong easterly wind makes it especially vulnerable. This enormous barrier spanning the Thames was built between 1972 and 1982 to protect the city from such a disaster. It consists of **11 massive gates** supported between vast concrete piers. The visitor center contains exhibits relating to the Barrier's history and various scenarios should London flood.

Sights Out of Town

Kew Gardens
Kew Road, Kew Surrey
Tel 0208 940 1171
www.rbgkew.org.uk
Gardens open daily 9.30am to
6.30pm. Glasshouses march to
October 9.30am to 5.30pm,
November to February 9.30am
to 4.15pm
Admission: £6.50
Nearest Tube: Kew

It's often forgotten that The **Royal Botanical Gardens** at Kew, in west London, are a major botanical **research institute**, containing more than 38,000 plant species in over 300 acres of public parkland. The Gardens were founded by Queen Caroline and Princess Augusta in the 18th century. Rapid expansion took place in the next century, when some of the huge **glasshouses** were built, containing all kinds of exotic species from all over the world, some 60,000 species, many of them quite rare. Among the attractions within the Gardens are the metal and glass **Palm House**, built in 1848, containing, as the name implies, a wondrous collection of tropical foliage. The beautiful **Water Lily House** is also a must-see.

A major disaster hit Kew in October 1987, when a major storm destroyed most of the trees, the same year as the Institute received a major boost with the opening of the ultra-modern **Princess of Wales Conservatory**, housing plants in ten different computer-controlled time zones, from east African savannah to Floridean swamp. The grounds are a popular attraction in their own right, especially the woodland nature reserve of **Queen Charlotte's Cottage**, a wooden summerhouse used by George III and his wife Charlotte, who died here in 1818. The ten-story high **Great Pagoda**, built in 1762 by William Chambers, is star attraction among the Gardens' temples and follies and the newly-restored **Kew Palace**, built in 1631 as the Dutch House, was once a favored royal residence of George III.

Kew is a fascinating place, esteemed not only as one of the world's great public gardens, but as an important scientific research center. Despite the distance from central London, it is easily accessible by Tube.

Richmond
Nearest Tube: Richmond.

Henry VII built a palace here in 1500 when it was just a small hamlet on the Thames, but today's Richmond is virtually a small town in its own right, with a busy high street typical of many English towns. But beyond the generally dreary facades of the main shopping streets are some lovely, elegant 18th century **town houses**, as well as the huge **Richmond Riverside** development, with classical facades designed to blend in with the other buildings around.

You may want to spend an hour or two browsing the many antique shops in Richmond, or take a stroll in **Richmond Park**, at 2,400 acres, the largest of all London's royal parks, established by Charles I in 1637 for the purposes of hunting. Mostly grassland and heath, it's home to dozens of wild red and fallow deer – and some ancient oak trees that probably oversaw the construction of **White Lodge**, built for George II in

1729 and now home of the Royal Ballet School. Or check out **Ham House** or **Marble Hill House** (see below). Rather than taking the tedious journey from central London to Richmond by Tube, why not hop on a **boat** from Westminster Pier?

Ham House
Ham Street, Richmond
Tel. 0208 940 1950
www.nationaltrust.org.uk
Open March to October Saturday to Wednesday 1pm to 5pm; November and December weekends 1pm to 5pm. January and February closed
Admission: £5
Nearest Tube: Richmond

West of **Richmond Park** is this lovely, 1610 home built by Sir Thomas Vavasour, knight marshal to James I. It was taken over later that century by the Duke and Duchess of Lauderdale, who transformed it into one of the finest houses in England of that time when it was at the heart of Restoration court life and intrigue. It was then occupied by the same family until 1948. Millions of pounds have recently been spent by the National Trust in restoring the house, and the result is stunning: the once-empty library has been redecorated and filled with 17th and 18th century books; the original decorations in the **Great Hall, Round Gallery and Great Staircase** have been replicated; and all the furniture and fittings have been restored. The formal garden is significant for its survival within the area known as the cradle of the English Landscape Movement. The outbuildings include an orangery, ice house, still house and dairy with cast iron 'cows legs' supporting marble slabs.

Marble Hill House
*Richmond Road, Twickenham
Tel. 0208 892 5115
www.english-heritage.org.uk/london
Open April to October, Saturdays 10am to 2pm, Sundays 10am to 5pm
Admission: £3.70
Nearest Tube: Richmond (a 25 minute walk away)*

Located on the picturesque Thames Path across the bridge from Richmond village, Marble Hill House is a beautiful Thames-side villa in the Palldian style, was built in the 1720s for Henrietta Howard, mistress of King George II. The intimate rooms give a glimpse of Henrietta's exuberant lifestyle; as well as connections to the court, she had close connections to the literary world of Jonathan swift and Alexander Pope.

Windsor Castle
*Brewhouse Yard, Windsor, Berkshire
Tel. 0175 367 1177
www.royal.gov.uk
Open November to February 9.45am to 4.15pm (last admission 3pm); March to October 9.45am to 5.15pm (last admission 4pm). Admission adults £10.50, seniors £8, Under-17s £5, under 5s free
Windsor is best accessed by train from London Waterloo (about 35 minutes).*

Windsor Castle was built 900 years ago by **William the Conqueror** to guard the western approaches to London. The site was chosen very carefully; high above the Thames, on the edge of a Saxon hunting ground and just a day's march from the Tower of London.

Today Windsor Castle is still a working palace, and the **State Apartments** contain some of the finest works of art, armor, paintings and decor in the world. Large sections of the Castle that were razed to the ground during the disastrous **fire of 1992** have now been completely rebuilt and refurbished to the highest standards. The work, which cost more than £37m (and caused a major furore when at first it was believed that all of the funds were to come out of the public purse), includes the restoration of the **Grand Reception Rooms**, **The Green and Crimson Drawing Rooms** and **the State and Octagonal Dining Rooms**. **St George's Hall**, where the Queen gives lavish banquets, had its ancient roof completely destroyed; today a brand new roof, built in the hammerbeam style like the old one, watches over the 600 year old hall.

Windsor Castle is so vast, it's only possible to touch on just a few of its major attractions here. As you enter, you can miss **St George's Chapel**, where the queen invests new knights and where various other important events take place – the wedding of the Queen's youngest son, Edward, to Sophie Rhys-Jones to name but one. Dating from the 15th and 16th centuries, when the Perpendicular style was in vogue, it contains beautiful **fan vaulting**, and beautifully carved choir stalls.

From the **North Terrace**, you can enjoy magnificent views across the Thames to the fa-mous **Eton College** (where Prince William was a student until summer 2000). From here, you enter the **State Apartments**, lavish beyond belief, with priceless antiques, Gobelin tapestries, old master paintings and even a Louis XVI bed. Also here are the **Throne Room**, and the **Waterloo Chamber**, where you can examine the set of paintings of Napoleon's foes which hang on the walls. Several items of armor are on show, and you can take a look at the superb **Queen's Collection of Master Drawings**, with works by Leonardo, and 87 Holbein portraits.

You should also take a look at **Queen Mary's Dolls' House**, left of the entrance to the State Apartments. Sir Edward Lutyens won the commission to create the Dolls' House in 1921, and it was completed in 1924. His goal was to "enable future generations to see how a King and Queen lived in the 20th century, and what authors, artists and craftsmen of note there were during their reign." The house was built on a scale of one to twelve and involved over 1,500 craftsmen.

At Windsor you can also see (another) **Changing of the**

Guard ceremony. This takes place daily (except Sundays) at 11am from April to the end of June, and on alternate days at other times of the year. Call *0175 386 8286* to confirm the times.

SPORT IN LONDON

England's national game, soccer (known as "football" here) is its most popular. The major clubs, Arsenal, Chelsea and Tottenham all pull in crowds of around 40,000 for home games. The national soccer stadium, Wembley, is being redeveloped and is due to re-open in 2005. Cricket is the summer game, and international matches, known as 'tests' are held at Lord's, in St John's Wood, and at the Oval in Kennington. Wimbledon is home of the All England Tennis Club and the famous Championships are held there in July. Rugby is popular; Twickenham in west London is the venue for England's international games. ❧

Hampton Court Palace
East Molesey
Tel. 0208 977 8441
www.hrp.org.uk

State Apartments open April to October Tuesday to Sunday 9.30am to 6pm; November to March Tuesday to Sunday 9.30am to 4.30pm, Monday 10.15 to 4.30pm
Admission adults £10, children £6.60. Grounds open 8am to dusk daily (free, but maze £3)
To get there: take a train from Waterloo to Hampton Court Station. Journey time: about 35 minutes

This is another beautiful **royal palace** – although no monarch has lived here since 1730 – about 20 miles west of the central London, just upstream from Richmond. The magnificent red-brick Tudor house was begun in 1514 under the auspices of the powerful **Cardinal Wolsey**, the nations' Lord Chancellor (which amounts to prime minister today), as well as being Archbishop of York. His desire to create the most lavish palace in the land upset Henry VIII so much that Wolsey felt obliged to give it to the king, and Henry moved in in 1525, spending a good deal of his time here.

Henry made some additions, including the **Great Hall and Chapel** but much greater expansion took place during the reign of William and Mary, who originally intended to demolish the Palace and replace it with an even grander affair, modelled on the palace of Versailles. Financial constraints meant that this was not possible, so Sir Christopher Wren was commissioned to extend the Palace to the rear, resulting in the construction of the very beautiful South Wing.

Start in the older part of the Palace at **Henry's Great Hall**, a massive area designed to make you feel small and intimidated, which in Henry's time was used mainly as a canteen where 600 men ate two meals daily. Its 60ft walls are covered with Flemish tapestries dating from 1540, illustrating the history of Abraham. The fan vaulted ceiling is impressive, too. **The Great Kitchen**, where the meals were prepared, was built in 1542 and has been painstakingly restored. In Henry's day it would have had a staff of over 200 men, women and children. The **Royal Chapel** is another part of the original Tudor building that remains virtually intact, but with additions by Wren and a reredos screen carved by Grinling Gibbons. There's a superb turquiose and gold fan-vaulted

ceiling painted by Sir James Thornhill.

To the left and right of Wren's Fountain Court are the **King's and Queen's Apartments**. **The King's Guard Chamber**, decorated as it was in 1699, has a display of 3,000 arms arranged in decorative patterns. This area would have accommodated up to 40 guards protecting the King.

The **Privy Chamber** was out of bounds to all but the Groom of the Stool (you can guess which stool this is). The highlight here is a beautiful ceiling illustrating Endymion asleep in the arms of Morpheus. A bad fire here in 1986 caused the ceiling and floor to collapse, leaving the chandelier in smithereens. Painstaking reconstruction of the chandelier using transparent glue means that today you cannot see any evidence of breakage. The **Orangery**, downstairs, is where William grew oranges (surprise!) and bay trees.

The location adjacent to the Thames is glorious, and allowed the monarch to get into central London very quickly by boat. The palace is full of priceless paintings, original furniture and – it is said – the ghost of **Catherine Howard**, protesting her innocence of the adultery that had her beheaded.

Outside, sixty acres of exquisite ornamental gardens are the perfect place to while away a few hours. If you have a few more hours (or days) to spare, you can explore the famous Hampton Court **Maze**, first planted in 1714. Or if you don't want to take that risk, take a stroll through the Elizabeth Know garden, stocked with medicinal and kitchen herbs, or check out the Great Vine, planted in 1768 for George II, still yielding around 600lbs of grapes. Don't miss the **Renaissance Picture Gallery**, used by Henry VIII to impress foreign dignitaries, with a collection of works by Holbein, Titian and Breughel's *Massacre of the Innocents* – one of the most terrifying paintings in existence. You can end on a more upbeat note with a visit to the Lower Orangery, where Mantegna's nine *Triumphs of Julius Caesar* are displayed. Commissioned in 1474, they were purchased for £10,500 by Charles I and have been restored recently.

ON PUBS

One of England's greatest assets is the pub. Pubs come in all shapes and sizes, and there's a pub for just about every mood and occasion. And they come with intriguing names, such as The King and Tinker and The Scarlet Pig, usually for good reason. Some pubs have wonderful architecture – such as the Salisbury in St. Martin's Lane with its wonderfully ornate wooden carvings and mirrors. Many pubs are franchises of a large brewery concern and sell that brewery's products. However, there is an increasing number of **free houses** that stock a wider variety of beers and wines – and often serve excellent, and inexpensive **food**.

You must be **over 18** to partake of alcohol in Britain; though children under-14 are often tolerated in pubs -always if they're eating – otherwise it's really is at the discretion of the landlord. Outdoor areas, such as **beer gardens**, are also child-friendly.

2. WALKS

London is a great city to go walking in. You can stroll by the River Thames, or you can wander in a wealth of green spaces, from the famous royal parks to large semi-rural areas like Hampstead Heath. The City of London with its medieval streets and alleyways begs to be explored on foot. In such a populated area a sense of solitude is rare, and traffic can be intrusive on London's notoriously congested streets. But to compensate there is the fascinating history and culture of one of the world's great cities, and facilities and services, including a good public transport network, near at hand.

THEATRELAND

London is the theatre capital of the world, with more than 500 venues. More than 50 of them are located within a relatively small area known as the West End. This walk gives you a brief introduction to the area.

*Start the walk at the theater ticket booth in Leicester Square, the hub of London's theater district. Leave the Square by Cranbourn Street, until you come to Charing Cross Road, with the **London Hippodrome** on you left. Turn right into Charing Cross Road.*

Immediately opposite is **Wyndham's Theatre**. It opened in 1899 and Madonna made her West End debut here in *Up for Grabs*. Stay on Charing Cross Road, passing the **Garrick Theatre** on your left. The Garrick, a nightmare to build because there's an underground river beneath it, dates from 1884. Its staple diet is comedies and comedy-dramas. The National Portrait Gallery follows almost immediately on your right.

Turn left into William IV Street, passing the graceful spire of St. Martin's-in-the-Fields, home of the Academy of St Martin-in-the-Fields, on your right. Cross St Martin's Lane.

On your left, the large building with the ball on top is the recently refurbished **London Coliseum**, home of the English National Opera. With 2,358 seats, it's one of London's largest auditoriums. The elegant cream-colored building on your right is the rear of Coutts Bank. Just past this building, on the right, is The Strand. Turn left into The Strand, passing Pizza Hut on your right. The **Adelphi** is just a few yards along on your left. One of London's oldest theatres, it opened in November, 1806 as the *Sans Pareil* before changing its name to Adelphi in 1819. In 1858 the theatre was replaced by a more up-to-date building now called New Adelphi and then Royal Adelphi in 1867. Just a few feet further on, the **Vaudeville** first opened on 16th April 1870 with the comedy *For Love or Money.*

About 300 feet further on, and on the opposite side of the road is the Savoy Hotel and Theatre, and then, Smollensky's Restaurant. You'll soon be passing two pubs – the Lyceum Tavern and the Duke of Wellington.

To your left, a few yards up Wellington Street, is the **Lyceum** whose early presentations included hot air balloon displays, an animal circus and fireworks. In 1802 Madame Tussaud's first exhibition of waxworks was held here. It burned down in 1830. Samuel Beazley designed the replacement. His magnificent portico still stands today. It was restored to its former glory in 1994.

Keep following The Strand where it forks to the left. Turn left into Catherine Street (poorly marked). You now pass the intimate Duchess Theatre, opened in 1929.

Productions ranging from Noel Coward's *Blithe Spirit* to *The Dirtiest Show in Town* have been staged here. On your right, the elegant **Theatre Royal** is said to be the oldest site in the world in continuous theatrical use. With its portico and colonnade, grand staircase and rotunda, it was the site for the first public rendition of *God Save the King*, in 1741, and *Rule! Britannia* nine years later. The theatre has hosted major musicals such as *The King and I* and *Miss Saigon.*

Turn left at the end into Russell Street, with the Fortune Theatre just behind you.

The Fortune (1924), an Art Deco gem, is where Kenneth More and Dirk Bogarde appeared early in their careers.

At the crossroads with Bow Street is, on your left, the The-atre Museum; on the right is the new extension to Covent Garden Opera House.

The original 1858 Opera House was recently refurbished to the tune of £220 million. You might want to spend a while exploring **Covent Garden Market**, for some timeout.

Otherwise turn right into Bow Street, with the main entrance to the Royal Opera House on your left, passing Bow Street police station on your right. Soon you come to a small rotary. Turn left into Long Acre, then right a few hundred feet later into Neal Street. Spend a bit of time exploring Neal's Yard, a hidden labyrinth of organic cafes, food shops and New Agey outlets. Stay on Neal Street, turning left at Shorts Gardens.

Soon you'll be at Seven Dials, another small rotary and home of the **Cambridge Theatre**, spiffed up for *Jerry Springer – The Musical.*

Take the third exit, Monmouth Street. Then turn right into West Street, with the main of-fices of the actor's union, Equity, on the corner.

Immediately on your right is the **St. Martin's Theatre** and the **New Ambassadors** which between them have hosted Agatha Christie's *The Mouse-trap* for over 50 years. The **West Street Chapel**, where John and Charles Wesley preached, is further along on the right.

Soon you reach Cambridge Cir-cus with the massive Palace Theatre, home for many years of Les Miserables, looming in front of you. Turn left into Shaftesbury Avenue, crossing Charing Cross Road. Down the side streets to your left is Chinatown.

On your right, in quick succession, come four theatres: the **Queen's**, **The Gielgud**, named after the distinguished actor Sir John Gielgud, who died in 2000 and previously known as *The Globe*. The Edwardian façade camouflages a regency building; an original staircase leads to the dress circle. This was the setting for Oscar Wilde's *The Importance of Being Earnest* in 1939, directed by and starring Gielgud himself. **The**

Apollo (1901) and **The Lyric** (1888) then follow.

Turn left at Great Windmill Street and on to Haymarket.

A few yards down Haymarket on the right is the **Comedy Theatre**, opened in 1881 as the *Royal Comedy*. Half way down on the left, is the **Theatre Royal** (1821), with its elegant Nash portico and the royal coat of arms over the entrance. **Her Majesty's Theatre**, with its palatial façade, is almost opposite.

Turn left into Pall Mall East, which leads into Trafalgar Square, keeping the National Gallery to your left. Just past the gallery turn left into Charing Cross Road, following it back to Leicester Square Tube station.

DIANA MEMORIAL WALK

Princess Diana knew London very well. A number of neighborhoods have close associations with her, including Pimlico, where she once worked as a nursery teacher and Kensington, where she lived after her divorce from Prince Charles. This walk takes us around another area, St James, famed for its expensive shops and chic restaurants and clubs. This is where London's smart set comes to see and be seen. We'll explore several of the streets Diana knew well, and visit shops and stores familiar to her.

The walk starts at **Piccadilly Circus Underground station**. Piccadilly Circus is famous for the bright lights of numerous advertisment hoardings, mostly on its northern side. But its main feature is the statue of the **Angel of Christian Charity** (not, as often supposed, Eros), erected in memory of the great 19th century philanthropist, Lord Shaftesbury.

Come out of the Tube station (exit Piccadilly south), and head west along Piccadilly.

Soon on your left you will pass the attractive Wren church of **St James' Piccadilly**, with an open air antiques market in its grounds. Further on is the famous food store, **Fortnum and Mason**, founded in 1707 as a humble grocery store. It has evolved into the most upmarket food store in Britain. Diana used to come to meet family and friends in its famous tea rooms. Staff would give her a table in the far corner so that she could not be spotted easily.

Continue along Piccadilly, pass-

ing Piccadilly Arcade, with the Royal Academy and then the Piccadilly Arcade's more illustrious sister, the Burlington Arcade, opposite.

The Arcade was constructed in 1819 by Lord Cavendish. It's one of the world's oldest – and most exclusive - indoor shopping malls. Wardens in top hats keep watch to ensure that none of the strict code of conduct is breached; so make sure you don't whistle, drop litter, spit or even run while you're here!

Continue to St. James's Street and turn left.

Just a few yards down, on the left, the building with the maps outside is **White's Gentlemen's Club**, opened in 1693. It's known as 'the father of all London's men's clubs'. The club's membership list reads like a national *Who's Who* and many royals, including Prince Charles, allegedly belong. St. James's Street is full of fascination: No. 3, Pickering Place, was the home of the **Texas Legation** before Texas became part of the US. Many of the shops hold royal warrants: No. 9, for example, **Lobb Shop**, is where the Queen, Prince Philip and Prince Charles get

their footwear, and at No 71, **Truefitt and Hill**, the the Queen's hubby gets his hair cut. Cross Jermyn Street, known for its fine quality shops, and take the next left, Ryder Street. Almost in front of you, on the corner with Bury Street, is **Longmire Jewellers**. Three royal warrants above its door indicate that the Queen and Duke of Edinburgh are customers. Diana's engagement ring, costing £30,000, and her wedding ring were bought by Prince Charles here.

Turn right into Bury Street, with its fine arts galleries and then right again into King Street which brings you back on to St James's Street. Turn left, passing Berry Bros and Rudd, wine merchants to the royal family since the seventeenth century, till you come to Pall Mall, with St James's Palace right in front of you.

The Palace, built by Henry VIII on the site of an old hospital for female lepers, was begun in 1532. A large stone window to the right of the gatehouse is part of the **Chapel Royal**. Diana's body was kept here before being moved to Kensington Palace the day before her funeral.

Turn left into Pall Mall for a moment to explore Crown Passage, a narrow alleyway a few yards on.

Accompanying several interesting shops is the **Red Lion Inn**, one of central London's oldest and most atmospheric pubs. It was a favourite drinking place of Charles II, an ancestor of Diana, who used to come here via a secret tunnel from St James's Palace for liaisons with his mistress, Nell Gwynne.

Return to Pall Mall and cross the road here. Head down Marlborough Road, just left of the palace.

This junction is the point where, at Princess Diana's funeral procession in 1997, the horse-drawn carriage which carried Diana's coffin stopped to allow Princes William and Harry, Prince Charles, Earl Spencer, Diana's brother, and Prince Philip, to join the procession. The coffin, draped in the royal standard, was accompanied by 12 escorts from the Welsh Guards. A simple bouquet of white roses and an envelope from Prince Harry inscribed 'Mummy' were placed on top. Pass, on your left, the **Queen's Chapel**, built in 1623 by

Inigo Jones, and on the right **Friary Court**, where the succession of new monarchs is proclaimed.

At the bottom of Marlborough Road, turn right into The Mall, the leafy boulevard leading to Buckingham Palace.

Clarence House, built in 1827 by John Nash, was, until her death, the residence of the Queen Mother. The House has recently become the home of Prince Charles who has had it extensively, and expensively, refurbished. The Queen lived here before being made Queen and Princess Anne was born here. Diana lived here too, moving in just prior to her wedding.

Continue along The Mall, crossing Stable Yard Road. Ahead of you, behind the stern-looking statue of Queen Victoria stands Buckingham Palace. But leave them for another time. Turn right at Queen's Walk, with Green Park on your left.

About 1,000 feet on the right, the imposing building with three female statues on its roof is **Spencer House**, the ancestral home of the Spencer (Diana's) family, built in 1766 by the first Earl Spencer. The Spencers became a powerful family thanks to success as sheep traders in the 15th century. Their power, wealth and influence increased because they backed the right side in the Wars of the Roses.

Continue to the top of the Queen's Walk to Piccadilly. Turn right here.

The large building on the right is the **Ritz Hotel**, owned by Mohammed Al-Fayed, father of Dodi Al-Fayed, a popular haunt of the rich and famous. Al-Fayed also owns its sister hotel the Ritz in Paris, from where Diana and Dodi headed out that fateful night in a car driven by Henri Paul. The London version opened in 1906 and is a wonderful place for afternoon tea. Diana used to come here frequently to meet friends.

Cross Piccadilly and head up Berkeley (pronounced Barclay) Street. At Berkeley Square, (where the famous nightingales sang), keep to the left hand side.

Look for **Annabel's**, a prestigious night spot. This was supposed to have been the venue for Prince Andrew's stag party before his wedding to Sarah Ferguson. According to legend, Diana and Fergie, both in fancy dress, gatecrashed the

party, only to find that it had been moved to another, secret address.

Further along the square, at the corner with Mount Street, is **Nicky Clarke's** *hairdressing salon.*

Diana was a regular customer, along with many other famous celebrities.

Cross Berkeley Square through the middle and continue straight on into Bruton Place.

Opposite Number 24, a blue plaque commemorates the house where the present Queen was born, though it has long disappeared.

Continue straight on and turn right into New Bond Street, the home of many swanky shops, stores and galleries. Continue along New Bond Street, which becomes Old Bond Street and turn left at Piccadilly

You'll pass, on your left, Albany Court Yard, with, at its far end, **The Albany**, an exclusive apartment block. Former residents have included J. B. Priestley and Aldous Huxley. Though it's hardly far from the madding crowd, actor Terence Stamp, a friend of Diana, lived here, and Diana used to visit him frequently until the press found out.

Re-trace your steps along Piccadilly and back to Piccadilly Circus Underground Station.

JACK THE KNIFE

Victorian London was a vast, sprawling metropolis, continually expanding in all directions. The area east of The City had always been London's poorest neighborhood, attracting swathes of immigrants fleeing persecution, starting with French Huguenots in the 17th century, right through to the burgeoning Bangaldeshi community of today. In the late 1800s, more than 900,000 people lived here, many of whom lived well below the poverty line, many in complete squalor, receiving just a pittance for long hours of work. Over half of all children died before their fifth birthday and prostitution and alcoholism were a way of life for many.

Today's East End, though speckled with upmarket residential areas, and overshadowed by the prosperous tower blocks of Docklands, remains largely the same as it was in Victorian times. Much of the area retains a strong working class feel, and poverty is still an issue. This is the London of Jack the Ripper, the notorious murderer who butchered at least five prostitutes during a five-week killing frenzy in the fall of 1888, during which the whole of London was gripped in fear. To this day, despite hundreds of theories, his identity remains a mystery. This walk takes us through a large chunk of the East End, including several of the murder sites.

The walk starts at Liverpool Street mainline train station. Coming out of the Station (Bishopsgate exit), cross the road, and turn left to Brushfield Street, the third street on the right.

You might want to stop for breakfast at Number 48, **S&M Café**, *Tel 0207 247 2252*, (S&M stands for sausage and mash), where a dozen varieties of 'bangers' are available, as well as a good selection of beverages.

Turn right at the end (Commercial Street).

If you want, take some time to explore **Spitalfields Market**, where there has been a fruit and vegetable market since the 12th century. It received a royal charter from Charles II.

Today the focus is on antiques, clothes and jewelry. Many local residents would have been employed here during The Ripper's time.

Continue along Commercial Street, passing Fashion Street and Lolesworth Close, where several of the victims lived, though redevelopment means there's virtually nothing left of the old street. Continue to Thrawl Street.

It was near here that The Ripper claimed his final victim, **Mary Jane Kelly**, on November 9, 1888. Younger than the other victims, Kelly, a prostitute, had spent that evening in the **Ten Bells** pub, where a witness, George Hutchinson, saw her pick up a client. He followed the couple back to Miller's Court. The next morning, her body was discovered by a shop assistant who went knocking at her door when she failed to turn up for work. Kelly's murder had been the most brutal of all The Ripper's five killings. Hutchinson was able to provide the police with a good description, but no-one was ever found.

Take the next turn on the right (Wentworth Street) then turn left at a block of apartments.

In the **doorway of these apartments** (Number 50, now blocked up), a piece of blood-stained apron was found, which matched the apron worn by the fourth victim. An anti-Semitic message written on the back of the fragment was obliterated by the police commissioner, despite protestations from officers at the scene. Was he really concerned about inflaming anti-Jewish feelings, or was there a more sinister motive behind his action? The precise contents of the message remain a mystery.

Turn left at Goulston Street, then right at New Goulston Street. Cross Middlesex Street and go up Gravel Lane opposite. Continue as it turns into Stoney Lane and at the end of Stoney Lane turn left into Houndsditch. Enter the 'subway' (underpass) at Exit 2, coming out at Exit 1, where you turn right and walk a few yards into Mitre Square.

A few yards into Mitre Square on the sidewalk the badly mutilated body of **Catherine Eddowes** was discovered on September 30, 1888 at 1.45am – the fourth victim. Eddowes had been released from custody by police just 45 minutes before her body was found.

Go through the Square, then turn left into Mitre Street to the end. Turn left into Aldgate High Street, and cross the road, passing St. Botolph's Church on the left.

Look out, opposite, for the **Hoop and Grapes** pub, one of the few surviving seventeenth century timber framed buildings in the city of London. It survived the 1666 Great Fire by a (singed) whisker, the flames petering out just before reaching the building, then a private home.

Continue along Aldgate High Street as far as the underpass, and follow the signs to Whitechapel High Street.

Walk along this street, passing, opposite, the famous **Whitechapel Art Gallery**, until you come to the junction with Plumber's Row, and the famous **Whitechapel Bell Foundry**. The Foundry has been here since 1570, but dates back even further, to 1420. The company has manufactured some of the world's best-known bells, including the Great Bell of Westminster, better known as Big Ben, and the original Liberty Bell of 1752. You could stop for a cup of coffee at *Café Casablanca*, on the opposite corner.

Continue along Whitechapel Road, passing a mosque on the right, until you come to the **Royal London Hospital**.

The hospital (founded 1740) is perhaps best known as the place where **Joseph Merrick – the 'Elephant Man'** – was treated and eventually died. He had been living in rooms at 259 Whitechapel Road.

Take the next left, Brady Street, and turn left again into Durward Street.

This is where on the night of August 30, 1888, the body of The Ripper's first victim, **Mary Ann Nichols**, was found. She had only been dead for 15 minutes or so, having had her abdomen ripped, and her throat cut twice – from left to right, indicating that her assailant was likely left-handed.

Continue straight on, then at the end turn right then first left along Old Montague Street (the sign says Hanbury Street, for some reason) as far as the junction with Osborn and Brick Lane. Turn right and continue along vibrant Brick Lane until you reach Hanbury Street, with its balti and tandoori restaurants. Turn left into Hanbury Street.

A small yard at the rear of **Number 29** (now part of Truman's Brewery) was the site of the discovery of the body of **Annie Chapman**, The Ripper's second victim, on Saturday September 8, at 6am. A man aged about 40, and wearing a deerstalker hat, was seen talking to Annie just minutes earlier. Was this Jack?

*Return to Brick Lane and turn right again down **Fournier Street**.*

This is one of the best-preserved eighteenth century terraced streets in London. Some of the houses – Number 7, for example – retain on their facades, the badges which indicated that the owner had signed up for fire insurance (these replaced homes that had been destroyed by the Great Fire). At the end of Fournier Street you will see the **Ten Bells** pub (mentioned earlier), built in 1753 and popular haunt of several of The Ripper's victims.

Spare a few moments to explore newly-restored **Christ Church**, built between 1714-1729, and one of architect Nicholas Hawksmoor's best, with its massive tower and soaring, elegant steeple. During an excavation in the crypt below the main church, workmen in 1980 discovered around 1,000 coffins all stacked up on top of one another, victims of smallpox. Because many of the bodies were in an advanced state of decomposition, builders had to wear white protective suits to prevent infection from the lethal spores.

Cross over to Brushfield Street and back to Liverpool Street station.

HAMPSTEAD HIKE

The great thing about Hampstead – at least certain parts of it – is that although you're only four miles from the West End, it can feel as if you're way out in the country. Even the more urban bits have more of the feel of an affluent English market town about them than that of a London suburb. This walk takes you through the best of both: some of the prettiest and most elegant streets in London, lovely rolling fields and semi-wild woodland – with a priceless art collection and a clutch of London's oldest pubs thrown in for good measure. There's even the opportunity for an open air swim if the weather is warm, so take your swimsuits and a towel! (See also the introduction to Hampstead in the Sights section)

*Take the Tube's Northern Line to Hampstead station - at 181ft below street level, London's deepest. Leaving the station, turn left on to **Hampstead High Street***

Here you'll find a motley collection of upmarket clothes stores, trendy cafes, bars and restaurants and even a cinema or two. Pop in to **The Dome** for a coffee, and then continue exploring the High Street.

*Keep going down the hill until you come to Downshire Hill. Turn left here, and continue past some very elegant Georgian houses to Keats Grove, and **Keats House**.*

The great romantic poet lived here from 1818 until his tragic death of consumption in 1820, at 25.

*Turn right at the end of Keats Grove, then first left to **Parliament Hill**.*

Climb the path at the end of the street for one of the best views of London. Look out for the Millennium Wheel, the Telecom Tower, the 'Gherkin' – Sir Norman Spencer's rocket-shaped skyscraper, and, further east (left) the high rise blocks of Canary Wharf.

*Follow the path towards the **Highgate Bathing Ponds**.*

This is a series of open air lakes used by Londoners to cool off on hot summer days. There are separate men's and women's ponds (the water flows through the women's first!)

*Continue north along the path, passing through wooded areas and following the signs (and asking directions, if necessary) for **Kenwood House**.*

This is a lovely 18th century country home with a very impressive small art collection, The **Iveagh Bequest**. For some time out, make for the adjacent **Coach House**. Its wide selection of refreshments, hot and cold, will keep you happy. If the weather's warm, the lawn running down from Kenwood House to the concert bowl is a great place for a picnic.

Behind the House take the path that leads off to the west. Eventually you will come to Hampstead Lane. Turn left here. Hampstead Lane becomes Spaniards Road.

Soon, on your right, is **The Spaniard's** pub. Past customers have included highwayman

Dick Turpin, and the poets Keats, Shelley and Byron.

Continue along Spaniards Lane to a rotary.

Here, **Jack Straw's Castle**, is another venerable pub, but unlike the Spaniards, much altered from when first built.

Turn left onto Heath Street, then right at The Mount, which brings you to Hampstead Grove.

You'll see beautiful, red-brick **Fenton House**, one of the finest in Hampstead. See the original main staircase, and a wonderful collection of early keyboard instruments dating from 1540.

Turn right on leaving the House and then right again on Frognal Rise, and left into Frognal. Number 99, on the left, is the former London residence of **General Charles de Gaulle**. *Continue down Frognal and turn left into* **Church Row**.

This is one of London's best preserved Georgian streets. The parish church of **St John**, built in 1745 is worth a glance; the painter John Constable is buried here.

Turn left at Heath Street, and very soon you will find yourself *back at Hampstead Tube Station.*

If you have a few minutes to spare, you could take a stroll down **Flask Walk**, just above the station - another disarmingly pretty street. It has a great pub – **The Flask** – with an attractive courtyard. A little further on, **Well Walk**, which takes its name from the well which provided clean drinking water to Hampstead, is where John Constable and D. H. Lawrence lived. Retrace your steps back to Hampstead Underground Station.

CHELSEA

It was in 1520 that Sir Thomas More moved to Chelsea, then nothing more than a small fishing village on the Thames. He was followed by several members of the aristocracy, including King Henry VIII. The place remained fairly obscure until the late 19th century, when the establishment of the Chelsea Arts Club (1891) started a trend towards a more bohemian lifestyle that Chelsea became noted for. This reached a peak in the 1960s, with pop stars like Mick Jagger and fashion designers like Vivian Westwood moving into the area, and Chelsea became the place to see and be seen. Things are a bit quieter today, but Chelsea is still a fascinating place, with some fine shops and restaurants, elegant town houses, and the Royal Hospital, home of the elderly war veterans affectionately known as the 'Chelsea pensioners.'

Start the walk at Sloane Square, Chelsea's Underground Station.

Sloane Square is named after Sir Hans Sloane, an 18th century naturalist and physician. His collection became the nucleus of the British Museum. The Square also gives its name to 'Sloane Rangers' – the debutantes of the 1980s, like Lady Diana Spencer and Lady Sarah Ferguson. Over to your right, the **Royal Court Theatre** saw the first performance of George Bernard Shaw's *Major Barbara*, and is dedicated to encouraging the work of new playwrights.

Cross the Square and follow the King's Road.

The huge **Peter Jones** department store – part of the John Lewis chain – is on your right. Number 152, King's Road, **The Pheasantry,** stands out with its fancy portico containing Grecian style statues. Pheas-

ants were once bred here, but from 1916 to 1936 it was a ballet school where Margot Fonteyn strutted her stuff. These days it's a trendy restaurant. This end of the King's Road has a number of fashion stores and boutiques, antiques stores and markets; **Antiquarius** at Number 135-141 is particularly worth a visit. **Flood Street**, on the left, is where Mrs Thatcher lived when not at Downing Street.

*Continue down the King's Road until you reach **Number 430**, about a mile from Sloane Square.*

Appropriately, a kink in the road heralds the spot where designer Vivienne Westwood and her then-boyfriend Malcolm MacLaren opened up a teddy boy revival store called **Let It Rock**. The shop's name changed to Sex in 1975, and became a magnet for the likes of Johnny Rotten and Sid Vicious from the Sex Pistols, who were drawn to its punk fetishist gear. The shop is known today as **World's End**, and though the burnt limbs that once graced the window display are long gone, you can still buy Westwood's innovative designs here. World's End, incidentally, is the name given to this part of

Chelsea by locals – because less swanky Fulham begins around here!

Turn left on to Old Church Street.

At the end, **Chelsea Old Church** (All Saints') is Sir Thomas More's old church, dating from the mid-13ᵗʰ century. Sir Thomas wouldn't sign the Oath of Supremacy to Henry VIII and paid the price with his life; he was executed as a traitor. A golden-faced statue of Sir Thomas sits on a throne looking towards the River.

*Turn left at **Cheyne Walk** (pronounced "chainy"), one of the best-known residential streets in London.*

A plaque at **Number 23**, for example, indicates the site of Henry VIII's Manor House, where his daughter Elizabeth (later Elizabeth I) lived from 1536 to 1547. Former Prime Minister Lloyd George lived at **Number 10**, Dante Gabriel Rossetti and Algernon Swinburne at **Number 16**, and George Eliot at **Number 4**. More recent members of the Cheyne gang have included Keith Richards of the Rolling Stones and J. Paul Getty. A statue of **Thomas Carlyle** marks the entrance to **Cheyne Row**, where he once lived. You can tour his house.

*Continue along Cheyne Walk to the **Albert Bridge**, built in 1873.*

The green wooden hut to the right of the bridge is a cabbie shelter – one of just a handful surviving of an original 61 – where cabbies can still get a hot meal.

Continue along Cheyne Walk and then fork left at Royal Hospital Road. Proceed to Swan Walk.

Here, give yourself some time to explore the **Chelsea Physic Garden**, first planted in 1673 and the oldest botanical garden in England after Oxford's.

*Head back on to Royal Hospital Road and stop for a moment at **Tite Street**..*

Famous residents of this street have included Oscar Wilde (**Number 34**), Augustus John (**33**) and James Whistler (**13**).

*A few yards further on, turn right to the **National Army Museum**.*

At this museum you can trace the history of British land

forces from the Yeomen of the Guard to the present day.

Head back on to Royal Hospital Road again.

The road takes its name from the magnificent **Royal Hospital**, founded in 1682 by Charles II as a hospital for infirm soldiers. Sir Christopher Wren was commissioned to design it; the result is a red brick and Portland stone masterpiece. The 400 or so navy-blue or scarlet uniformed veterans – **Chelsea pensioners** – who reside here have some wonderful stories to tell, and might even be persuaded to show you round Wren's lovely **Chapel and Great Hall**.

As you continue north east along Royal Hospital Road turn left at Frankin's Row, and left again into St. Leonard's Terrace.

Number 18 was the home of the author of *Dracula*, Bram Stoker..

Turn right at Royal Avenue, the 'home' of Ian Fleming's fictional hero, James Bond, and back on to the King's Road. Turn right again, and back to Sloane Square Underground station.

3. MISCELLANY

AIRPORT INFO
Arrivals

Most transatlantic flights arrive at either **Heathrow**, *www.baa.co.uk,* about 15 miles west of the city, or **Gatwick** www.baa.co.uk) about 25 miles south. Once you've cleared customs and immigration (be prepared for your first experience of a British queue here) and you've picked up your baggage, there are a number of options for getting into downtown London:

Getting Into London

The most expensive way to travel is also the most exciting; an encounter with that rare and very special breed, the London taxi driver, or "cabbie." Drivers of the famous **black cabs** (some of them are now maroon) have to undergo extensive tests over a period of four years before they qualify and can claim to have "the Knowledge" – tell them the address you want, and they'll know exactly where it is. Usually. The ride from Heathrow will cost somewhere in the region of £35; from Gatwick £45 and up.

Mini cabs often operate a fixed rate – usually about £25 – for travel into central London. Confirm the price before you start your journey and avoid drivers touting for trade at the airport. Some companies offer **shuttle bus** services from the airports direct to your hotel. Among the best are **Airport Transfers** *(Tel. 020 7403 2228)* and **Hotelink** *(Tel. 01293 532244),* who charge £12 per person to the West End from Heathrow and £18 from Gatwick. Tipping for all taxi drivers is customarily 10%.

You can also go by train: the **Heathrow Express** *(Tel. 08456 001515)* runs up to four trains an hour to the Airport from Paddington Train Station. Fares start at around £13.

By Bus:National Express *(Tel. 08705 757747)* run services from Victoria Bus Station and from King's Cross Train Station. Fares start at £10.

By **Underground**: The Piccadilly Line connects Heathrow with central London. Trains run every five to ten minutes and fares are £3.60 for adults, £1.50 for children. London Underground's **Piccadilly line** extends west to Heathrow, connecting the airport with such central destinations as Piccadilly Circus and Leicester Square (and around 20 other stops on the way!) The ride into central London takes around 45 minutes, and costs £3.50. If you're going to be using the Underground later on in the day, it makes sense to buy **a One Day Travelcard, zones 1-6**, which will get you around most of the System for £5.

GETTING AROUND

The Underground (Tube)
This is by far the quickest way to get around London (unless there are track, signaling or staffing problems in which case London Transport is usually very good at posting information at the entrance to the stations). Each of the 12 underground lines is color-coded.

Look for your destination on an Underground map, then figure out the most logical way to get there. You'll need to know the final destination on your chosen line (which is marked on the front of the train and on the overhead illuminated display) and the general direction (north, south, east or west) that the train is traveling. It may sound complicated, but it won't take long to get the hang of it.

Trains normally run from around 5am to midnight. Don't lose your ticket – or you might have to pay a hefty fine. Many destinations to the east of the City of London are covered by the Docklands Light Railway (DLR).

Renting a Car
Are you crazy?! Not only do the Brits drive on the wrong side of the road, there's a totally different driving culture and parking is a nightmare. Petrol (gas), due to government taxes, works out at least five times as expensive as it does in the US.

Boats
In olden days, the Thames was London's main thoroughfare, and on a sunny spring or summer's day there's nothing better than a trip on the

Thames, whether it's with a specific destination in mind (like Greenwich, Richmond or the Thames Barrier) just for the fun of it, or an evening supper cruise. For information about river trips, call the London Tourist Board's **River Trips Phoneline**, *Tel. 0839 123 432*, or just show up at Westminster Pier, just below Big Ben.

Buses

London's red **double-decker buses** are familiar to everyone, a great way of getting round the city, and, occasionally, of striking up conversation with the locals. Maps of London's bus routes are available from **London Transport**, *Tel. 0207 222 1234*, and at most Underground stations, but if you have a particular destination in mind, don't hesitate to phone them and ask for the best way of getting there. Older buses come with conductors, who have an amazing knack of knowing who hasn't paid their fare. They'll often (but not always, they sometimes forget) will point out your destination stop to you if you ask nicely. Newer buses tend to be one-person operated, so be sure you have your fare ready (tip: bus drivers hate to be given large bills for small fares; you might not even be able to get on the bus if you don't have change). When you see your bus approaching, put out your arm as if hailing a taxi. Buses are not the quickest way of getting around London – though the introduction of bus-only lanes has helped a great deal – but you can enjoy great views (especially from the top deck).

Night buses are a useful way of getting home late at night, after the Tube has shut down, though there are disadvantages: they don't accept travelcards, and you might end up singing rugby songs with a load of drunks. Most night buses run hourly through the night; Trafalgar Square tends to be a good place to catch one.

Maps

London's layout is, to say the least, complicated, so don't try to navigate London without a decent map. The maps they give you at the tourist center are fine for getting to the basic sights, but for just £5 you can buy an **A to Z** (pronounced "Zed"), which even Londoners use to get around. They include an enlarged map of the central area and an underground map.

Taxis

London taxis are spacious, the drivers - cabbies - usually real characters, and you can count on getting to your destination in the shortest possible time (drivers are short cut experts). If you're hailing a cab, look for one with an illuminated amber light on top; it's available for hire. Put out your arm, and tell the driver the destination you want. All journeys are metered. When you pay, don't forget the 10% (at least) tip. Minicabs are available throughout London, and are generally slightly cheaper than the traditional black cabs, but I wouldn't recommend picking one out of a list in yellow pages or on an advertisement. Ask your hotel if they can recommend a company.

Buying Tickets

London's transport system is the most extensive – and expensive – in Europe, but bear a few things in mind and you can cut your losses. A one-day **travelcard** can be used on all buses and Underground trains in the zones specified (except night buses) for a flat fare. If you're going to be making two or more bus/Underground journeys on any one day, it makes a great deal of sense to purchase one. Weekly and monthly travelcards are also available; for the latter, two photo booth-size snaps are necessary. Family travel cards can work out even more cheaply – but check your sums first.

Children under five travel free; 5-15s travel at reduced cost (until 10pm, when they are charged as adults on buses). 14 and 15 year-olds will need to carry a Child-Rate Photocard as proof of age, available at post offices.

If you're traveling without a travelcard, you'll need a single or round-trip ticket (called 'return' here). Check the cost of your journey to your destination at the station. Purchase the ticket at one of the automated machines, or the ticket office. Make sure you have paid the correct fare – travel one stop too far, and you may not be able to get through the exit barrier and you could be charged excess. And don't lose your ticket – you'll need it to exit the system.

Trains

While it's likely that you're staying at a fairly central location and won't need the train, they can come in very handy for getting to out-of-town attractions such as Windsor and

Hampton Court. For rail information, call *0345 484950*. See the Sights section for information about the Eurostar train to Paris.

USEFUL INFORMATION
American Express operates several branches in London. One of the most central is the office at 6, Haymarket (near Piccadilly Circus), *Tel 020 7930 4411*. **Thomas Cook** also has a large number of branches throughout the city.

Banks are generally open from 9.30am to 3.30pm, Monday to Friday, with some opening on Saturday mornings. Most ATM machines are open 24 hours a day and accept overseas cards with a Yankee 24 or Cirrus symbol. If you use one of the myriad bureaux de change throughout the city, make sure you check their commission rates before parting with your dollars; some of them charge extortionate fees.

The **electrical current** in London is 220/240 volts as opposed to 110 volts in North America. Don't melt your electric razor, hairdryer or laptop. You'll need a converter and an adapter. Some laptops don't require a converter.

The **US Embassy** in London is located at Grosvenor Square, *Tel. 0207 499 9000*, as is the **Canadian High Commission**, *Tel. 0207 258 6600*.

Dialing *999* anywhere in the UK will gives direct access to **emergency** – police, fire, ambulance or coastguard services - at any time of day or night. You can get emergency medical information by calling NHS Direct (24-hour advice line), *Tel. 0845 4647*. **MediCentre**, *Tel. 08706 000870*, operates Healthcare clinics throughout central London. Free emergency dental treatment is available at **Guy's Hospital Dental School** *Tel. 0207 955 5000*. Privately-run services include:
- **Doctorcall**, *Tel 07000 372255*
- **Medcall**, *Tel. 0800 136106*
- **Opticall**, *Tel. 0207 495 4915*.

You'll need a valid **passport** to enter the UK. If you want to stay more than 90 days, you'll need a visa.

Late-opening **pharmacists** (chemists) are located at 5 Marble Arch: **Bliss** – open to midnight, *Tel 0207 723 6116*), and at Piccadilly Circus: **Boots** – open till 8pm, *Tel 0207 734 6125*.

Report **lost items** to your nearest police station. **London Transport** have a lost property office at 200 Baker Street, NW1, *Tel. 020 7486 2496.* The **Black Cab Lost Property Office** is on *0207 918 2000.* The Lost Property offices at **Heathrow Airport** is *Tel. 020 8745 7727.* Lost your credit card? Call **American Express**, *Tel. 01273 696933,* **Diners Club**, *Tel. 01252 513500,* **Mastercard/Visa**, *Tel. 01268 298178.*

The unit of **currency** is the pound sterling (£) which is divided into 100 pence. The pound comes only as a coin. Bills (notes) are £5, £10, and £50. Currency is available in larger travel agents, like American Express and Thomas Cook, at some hotels and post offices, as well as independent Bureaux de Change. An easier (and sometimes cheaper) option is to use an ATM; there are thousands all over the city. Credit cards (MC, Visa, American Express etc) are widely accepted at hotels, restaurants and stores. Travelers' checks can be used to obtain currency at banks, hotels and bureaux de change, but expect a frown if you attempt to make a purchase with them in a store or restaurant –

Brits never use them as cash. VAT is charged at 17.5% on many items; refunds can be obtained from some stores. International money transfer is available from **Western Union**, *Tel 0800 833833.*

Banks and businesses are generally closed on England's **public holidays** (known as **Bank Holidays**). Visitor attractions almost always close for Christmas Day and Boxing Day, but stay open on other holidays.
- Jan 1 *New Year's Day*
- Late March/April *Good Friday*
- Late March/April *Easter Monday*
- First Monday in May *May Day Bank Holiday*
- Last Monday in May *Spring Bank Holiday*
- Last Monday in August *Summer Bank Holiday*
- December 25 *Christmas Day*
- December 26 *Boxing Day*

London is on the whole very **safe**, but as with any of the world's large cities, a few common sense precautions will make it even safer: Avoid wearing a fanny pack. It's obvious you're a tourist and makes you an easy target. Wearing flashy jewelry is another enticement to would-be thieves. Never keep your wallet in the back pocket of your pants.

Public telephones take coins or telephone cards (obtainable at newsstands and post offices) or, increasingly, credit cards. Many also provide internet access. For **Directory Enquiries** (Directory Assistance) call *118 500* (for national calls) or *153* (international). There are many **internet cafes** throughout the city. When telephoning the UK from the USA or Canada, dial *011 44* followed by the UK number minus its initial '0'. So the UK number *01202 720848* becomes *011 44 1202 720848*.

Standard **tipping** policys is:
- Restaurants: usually 10-15% (only if it hasn't already been included in the check (bill)
- Taxis: 10% or round up to the nearest £
- Porters: £2 per bag

Tourist Information offices:
- Britain and London Visitor Centre, 1 Regent Street (no phone). Open Monday to Friday 9.30am to 6.30pm; weekends 10am to 4pm. Nearest Tube: Piccadilly Circus

- City of London, St Paul's Churchyard, EC4, Tel. 020 7332 1456. Open Monday to Friday 9.30am to 5pm, Saturdays 9.30am to 12.30pm. Nearest Tube: St Paul's
- Greenwich, Cutty Sark Gardens, SE10, Tel 020 88858 6376. Nearest train station: Greenwich
- Southwark, 1 Bank End, SE1. Nearest Tube: London Bridge
- London Tourist Board, Victoria Station Forecourt (no phone).

HOTEL TIPS
Prices for a double room

Expensive
(over £200)
Claridges
Brook Street, W1
Tel. 0207 499 2210
Nearest Tube:
Bond Street

The Dorchester
Park Lane, W1
Tel. 0207 629 8888
Nearest Tube:
Hyde Park Corner

The Ritz
Piccadilly, W1.
Tel. 0207 493 8181
Nearest Tube:
Green Park

The Savoy
The Strand, WC2
Tel. 0207 836 4343
Nearest Tube:
Covent Garden

Moderate
(£125 to £200)
Dorset Square Hotel
39 Dorset Square, NW1
Tel 0207 723 7874
Nearest Tube:
Baker Street

Durrant's
George Street, W1
Tel 0207 935 8131
Nearest Tube:
Bond Street

The Executive Hotel
57 Pont Street, SW1
Tel 0207 581 2424
Nearest Tube:
Knightsbridge

John Howard Hotel
4 Queen's Gate, SW7
Tel 0207 581 3011
Nearest Tube:
Gloucester Road

Inexpensive
The Elizabeth
37 Eccleston Square,
SW1
Tel 0207 828 6812
Nearest Tube: Victoria

James House
108 Ebury Street, SW1
Tel 0207 730 7338
Nearest Tube: Victoria

Regent Palace
Glasshouse Street
Piccadilly Circus, W1
Tel. 0870 400 8703
Nearest Tune:
Piccadilly Circus

The Windermere
142 Warwick Way,
SW1
Tel 0207 834 5163
Nearest Tube: Victoria

LANGUAGE TIPS

There are enough differences between 'English English' and 'American English' to result in the occasional crossed wire. Some words and phrases have quite a different, sometimes embarrassing connotation from their US or Canadian equivalent. And other words you'll have never heard before. Then there's the accents…

English English/American English

Aubergine/*eggplant*
The bill/*the check*
Biscuit/*cookie*
Boot/*trunk (car)*
Cot/*crib*
Courgette/*zucchini*
Dummy/*pacifier*
Engaged/*busy (phone)*
Football/*soccer*
Homely/*pleasant, comfortable*
Jumper/*sweater*
Lift/*elevator*
Loo/toilet/*bathroom*
Lorry/*truck*
Mean/*stingy*
Nappy/*diaper*
Newsagent/*newsstand*
Note/*bill (money)*
Pavement/*sidewalk*
Petrol/*gas (car)*
Queue/*line*
Roundabout/*rotary*
Rubber/*eraser*
Trousers/*pants*
Windscreen/*windshield*

INDEX

THINGS CHANGE!
Phone numbers, prices, addresses, quality of food, etc, all change. If you come across any new information, we'd appreciate hearing from you. No item is too small! Drop us an email note at: Jopenroad@aol.com, or write us at:

London Made Easy
Open Road Publishing, P.O. Box 284
Cold Spring Harbor, NY 11724

OPEN ROAD PUBLISHING

Look for all of Open Road's *new* European travel and menu-reader guides:

- Paris Made Easy, $9.95
- London Made Easy, $9.95
- Rome Made Easy, $9.95 (Spring 2005)
- Provence Made Easy, $9.95 (Spring 2005)
- Amsterdam Made Easy, $9.95 (Summer 2005)
- Eating & Drinking in Paris, $9.95
- Eating & Drinking in Italy, $9.95
- Eating & Drinking in Spain, $9.95

For US orders, include $4.00 for postage and handling for the first book ordered; for each additional book, add $1.00. Orders outside US, inquire first about shipping charges (money order payable in US dollars on US banks only for overseas shipments). Send to:

Open Road Publishing
PO Box 284, Cold Spring Harbor, NY 11724

New European Guides